CANADA
and the
UNITED STATES —

The Second Hundred Years

CANADA
and the
UNITED STATES—
The Second Hundred Years

by Stanley R. Tupper
and Douglas L. Bailey

Hawthorn Books, Inc.   *Publishers*   New York

1088

Acknowledgments

Dr. Bailey and I wish to express our deep appreciation to Miss Kathy Nelson, a graduate student in the Foreign Service School at Georgetown University, and Miss Tonnie Schwartz, a recent graduate of Barnard College, Columbia University. These two young ladies gave unstintingly of their time and talent in conducting research on various aspects of U.S.-Canadian relations.

Our thanks are also extended to Mr. Robert Coates of Amherst, Nova Scotia. Mr. Coates, a distinguished Member of the Canadian Parliament, gave generously of his time in obtaining data from a large number of Canadian secondary-school students. This material was most helpful in this undertaking.

We are also indebted to a long list of generous people who either aided in or helped to guide the research effort on some subjects treated in the book. They include The Hon. Paul Tremblay, Canadian Ambassador to Belgium and former Canadian Ambassador to the United Nations; Canadian-born Dr. Thomas Peardon, Professor Emeritus of Government at Columbia University; Mr. H. W. Thomson, Officer-in-Charge of the Canadian Government Immigration Service, New York City; Dr. Arthur A. Hauck, former President of the University of Maine; Dr. Sperry Lea, Executive Director of the Canadian-American Committee; Professor Chilton Williamson of Columbia University; Miss Virginia Brewer and Mr. Elden E. Billings of the U.S. Library of Congress; Mr. Andrew E. Kauders, assistant to Dr. Bailey; and the Staff of the Canadian Consulate-General in New York City, especially Miss Margaret Smith, Chief Research Librarian.

During three terms of Congressional service, I have been greatly disturbed over the noticeable lack of awareness by U.S.

5

citizens of Canada and its institutions. I felt there was an urgent need for a comprehensive analysis of the relationship between the two countries as well as for specific suggestions for improving that relationship in future years.

If this book results in stimulating more interest within the U.S. concerning our northern neighbor and helps Canadians to understand us better, Dr. Bailey and I will consider the effort well worth while.

Stanley R. Tupper

Preface

If there had been Americans like Congressman Tupper one hundred years ago we might never have had Confederation. We required screaming editors in New York and Montreal, Confederate raiders in Canada and Fenians in the States, braggart generals and all the talk of Manifest Destiny to unite the scattered British North American colonies. Like all new states, we needed this external threat for our coagulation, and for a good many years Americans performed the helpful service of scaring us into a miraculous confederation from the Atlantic to the Pacific. The threat was all the more real because the agents were waves of settlers rather than waves of Marines.

Americans like Congressman Tupper and Dr. Bailey would have subverted us in the nineteenth century with their abjuration of Manifest Destiny and their insistence on the advantages to the United States of Canada's independence in word and deed as well as in law. In the one hundredth year of the Confederation we can stand this sort of thing. Indeed, we welcome it gratefully. We have passed from the days when the *raison d'être* of the Canadian state was a sheltering together of those who for assorted reasons did not want to be republican Americans. Three hundred years and more of history (for Canada is a good deal older than its Confederation) have given us a sense of political identity and a satisfaction with our peculiar kind of country which makes our national feeling less defensive and more assertive. Our Canadianism gets a healthy stimulus from time to time when we stand together against aggression from the First National City Bank or Senator Wayne Morse, but we know that our protection lies in the institution of civilized discussion and negotiation, the development of which is the main theme of this wise book.

The authors bend backward to be fair to Canadians (the

Canadian reader should blush on occasion) and they are harsh toward their fellow countrymen. They are too sophisticated to give us the "great little country" treatment, to imagine that, in the complex and treacherous relations between a large and a small power with a huge border, good will can be a substitute for understanding based on homework. They have kept up their own homework. Their complaint is that from neither their newspapers nor their universities can Americans learn much about Canada, and that such ignorance is dangerous. A Canadian must agree with this stricture while acknowledging that the United States is much more important to him than Canada is to an American. We shall all need cool heads and knowledge both broad and deep if we are to continue managing our relations like the civilized people we are, for we are going to impinge on each other much more in the second century than we did in the first—not only in the Columbia but in the Mekong and other far-flung valleys. There is no such thing as settling the Canadian-American problem; there is the more exciting prospect of riding it.

There is so much to agree with in this sensitive, perceptive and well researched study that one hesitates to dispute with the authors at all. I might propose a footnote to the statement that the major obstacle to good relations is the American failure to think of Canada as an independent country. One reason for this lapse is that many Canadians don't think of their country as independent either. Canadians become so caught up, for example, in the civil rights movement that they parade in Alabama without reflecting on the impropriety of such foreign intervention. Such is the inequality of expression accorded large and small states, however, that no such liberty to tell Canada what to do is vouchsafed American citizens or the United States Government. Our Ministers have always felt free to make in American cities speeches wise with recommendations for United States policy, but when President Kennedy gently suggested in Ottawa that Canada would be welcome in the OAS, a storm blew up over this "interference." That is not fair, but it is a fact of life, and Americans had better not expect reciprocity in all things. It is one of the many disadvantages of being a great power.

The authors argue that a growing American awareness of Canada is dependent on Canada's capacity to define its own identity. This is fair comment, but it is a product of United States tradition and I hope the authors won't press us. The American mission was to create the American man; he has been a great success and we have all learned much from him. But Americans should not expect us to be a national state as they are, because that is not what we are cut out for. We must be accepted as different not only in what we do but in what we are and what we strive to be. For us the search for a unifying national character and for unity as an end in itself is sterile. It is not a quest which belongs to this century anyway. Our proper concern is to nourish and strengthen a constitutional framework where the freest of peoples find expression and protection and a high standard of living. As the world becomes more populous and closely knit, loose countries like Canada become more necessary.

There is only one other perspective of the authors that I would question, and that is the assumption that in the Western Hemisphere we inhabit the "New World," that Canada must shake off the "Old World" if it is to fulfill its destiny. This reflects an ambivalence many Canadians did feel once when the imperial tie to Britain inhibited our national imagination—more than it ever inhibited our freedom of action. Need we cast off as anachronistic a modern Commonwealth which we Canadians have to a large extent created, which has more "new" countries in it than the Organization of American States, whose strength and weakness is that it may be too progressive for the present state of mankind?

It is perhaps natural for Americans to assume that we shall never be weaned until we have severed our ties with the British Empire, as they did two centuries ago. But we profited from their experience and followed a different course. It was

9

more than just a question of gaining our independence by evolution rather than revolution; we did much more than that; we converted the Empire in the process into a Commonwealth of free peoples which has, by providing a framework for peaceful transformation of colonies to independence, spared the world —including the United States—much bloodshed.

The view of the hemispheres as "Old" and "New" seems more appropriate to the days before the United States itself had burst from hemispheric isolationism to become a powerful force all over the world. Canadians have no illusions about being a great power, but even as a lesser power they feel obliged as world citizens and members of the United Nations to be a "world" lesser power rather than a "continental" lesser power.

These opinions, I trust, the authors will accept merely as manifestations of that independent Canadian perspective—or that stubborn perversity—which they are so generously prepared to say is a good thing. They have done all Canadians a great service by extending the bounds of the great unfortified debate which Canadians can continue to enjoy with a tranquillity denied to most "smaller neighbors."

JOHN W. HOLMES

Toronto, Canada

10

Contents

CANADA
and the
UNITED STATES —

The Second Hundred Years

Chapter I

One Hundred Years Back, One Hundred Years Forward

This book is about North America—its opportunity and its obligation.

Ours is a continent blessed by God with abundance, by wise men with democracy, and by geography with time to develop them both. Today it is blessed with the opportunity—or perhaps damned by the obligation—to provide a model for relations between independent nations.

If Canada and the United States cannot channel the wonders of the technological revolution for the good of men; if Canada and the United States cannot build the social and economic patterns by which powerful neighbors can live at peace; if Canada and the United States cannot create mutual political institutions which will allow man to survive in the nuclear age, then which nations can?

This then is our theme: The obligation of our two countries to make of the North American continent a model for relations between independent nations is no less than our opportunity to do so. The one-hundredth anniversary of Canadian Confederation is 1967. Canadians will quite naturally pause to review their century and to dream of their future. But as 1867 saw the birth of a great nation, perhaps 1967 can see the birth of a continental design to shape man's future to man's dreams. We hope that the people of the United States will view 1967 as the year of a new awareness of Canada—its land, its people, its future—and we hope that both peoples will come to see their opportunity and their obligation as one and the same.

Two hundred years ago, Britain debated the choice between a colony in Canada and a colony on the Caribbean island of Guadeloupe. The Earl of Hardwicke's contribution to that debate showed that vision was no easier to come by then than now:

> Canada is a cold northern climate, unfruitful; furnishes no trade to Europe that I know of, but the fur trade, the most inconsiderable of all trades; and therefore never compensated to France the expense of maintaining and defending it. Its products are mostly or nearly of the same kind with those of Great Britain and consequently will take off not much of our's. Besides, if you remove the French inhabitants, this Kingdom and Ireland cannot furnish, or procure, people enough to settle and inhabit it in centuries to come; and, if you don't remove the French inhabitants, they will never become half subjects, and this country must maintain an army there to keep them in subjection.[1]

The attitude in the United States toward Canada in the early years of its independence nearly two hundred years ago was quite different—different from that of the British, but not different from what many Canadians may think of United States motives today. We wanted Canada. In informal negotiations at the close of the American Revolutionary War, Benjamin Franklin suggested to a British diplomat that whereas the United States might not demand Canada as a term of the settlement, "on the mind of the people in general, would it not have an excellent effect if Britain should voluntarily offer to give up this province." [2]

What most Americans* coveted two hundred years ago, many

* All the people who live in North America, or in South America for that matter, are "Americans." Those who have reviewed this manuscript before publication have warned its authors that some Canadians might resent our repeated reference to U.S. citizens, but not Canadians, as "Americans"—as if that term were descriptive of nationality.
For the sake of simplicity, we have, however, had to follow that course.

16

Americans demanded a hundred years ago. In 1870, Senator Zachariah Chandler, of Michigan, introduced a resolution to request the President to appoint negotiators to discuss with officials of Winnipeg the annexation of Canada. During the debate, Chandler declared boldly: "This continent is ours and we may as well notify the world . . . that we will fight for our own if we must." [3] And it is undoubtedly true that the threat of annexation by the United States was an important impetus to the confederation and formation of the Dominion of Canada in 1867.

Still another hundred years later, in 1967, American attitudes seem to have changed. Undoubtedly many Canadians would say merely that the change is that the United States no longer wants Canada: It merely wants to dominate its economy, to influence its vote at the United Nations, to take its water, and to use it as a buffer in a cold or nuclear war. The United States has long since lost its zeal for annexation, but in a real sense the common American attitude toward Canada today is no less cavalier and no less infuriating to Canadians than it was a century ago.

The nature of relations a hundred years from now, in 2067, will depend in great measure on the improvement of the psychological relations between the two states and the two peoples. If Americans continue to take Canada for granted, and if Canadians continue to be suspicious of every American initiative, progress will be thwarted, opportunity abandoned, and obligation ignored.

It is surely not unique to suggest that the U.S.–Canadian relationship is unique. But the truth of truisms should not be dismissed. No two neighbors ever shared a more compatible cultural heritage; no two neighbors ever shared a longer unfortified boundary; no two neighbors ever shared so many years of relative peace and harmony. All this we have heard endlessly before. But because of it, and because of the unique abundance which we also share, no two neighbors ever shared the opportunity which is ours to grow in material and political

17

progress—in establishing a model for relations between independent nations.

And from all this, our two nations, as none before, share the obligation to chart the paths of international behavior which can preserve this world intact in the coming years of relentless power and peril.

What are the statistics of the opportunity? In the last hundred years the population of North America grew from 40 million to 210 million; a hundred years from now the population could easily be over 1 billion. In the Canada of 1867, "west of the Great Lakes, white man, Indian, and half-breed, all told counted few more than a hundred thousand souls." [4] In the United States a hundred years ago, the energy so tragically wasted in a Civil War was turned to the development of the West so recently opened. Today we have fully mapped our lands, we know them and their resources. In a hundred years we can develop them. We can turn them to man's use. As nowhere else on earth, we have the richness of soil and space to accommodate this fantastic growth in population and to assure to every family not just shelter and food, but a home and the comforts of a civilization undreamed of in 1867, or even today.

One hundred years ago, the new Dominion Government took pride in less than 2,500 miles of railroad track. Today there are 45,000 miles of railroad track in Canada. The last hundred years have seen U.S. railroad track grow from 39,050 miles to 214,387 miles. One hundred years ago, there were no telephones, no radios, no television sets, no automobiles, and no airplanes. Today there are 95 million telephones in North America, 195 million radios, 66 million television sets, 78 million automobiles, and 250,000 miles of commercial airline routes. In 2067, perhaps the railroad, the automobile, and the airplane will seem as obsolete as the horse and buggy seem now. The telephone, the radio, and television may all have given way to fantastic new means of communication.

Both Canada and the United States have emerged as nations

during one hundred years of extraordinary technological achievement through which man can now know instantly of events in far-flung parts of his country and the world—and can be there soon after. Communications and mobility have built in these two spacious lands two peoples, each united as they could never have been a hundred short years ago.

If the communications of tomorrow and the mobility of tomorrow continue to grow as they have, the world of 2067 will be as unimaginable for us as the world of today was a hundred years ago. Man may commute thousands of miles in a moment to his job—or perhaps he will perform his job at home through the buttons of computers. Instant visual and audial communication with any part of the world (or perhaps our solar system) will be possible at the flip of a switch. It will be possible not merely to see the great events in the world as they unfold—but to be there as well. Today's networks of power grids will give way to world-wide grids of knowledge—for medicine, for agriculture, for education.

One hundred years ago the Canadian gross national product was $419 million and the U.S. was $6.71 billion. Today they are $51.5 billion and $675.5 billion respectively. (All figures are in U.S. dollars.) There is no reason to believe that they will not continue to grow in a geometric proportion until, one hundred years from now, the economic power of each of our nations—and certainly together—can command for all our citizens a veritable utopian existence. In each of our countries, the greatest problems will not be the adequate employment of all but the productive utilization of leisure time.

The question to be asked as we look forward to this glowing experiment in material abundance is whether the social, economic, and political institutions in and between our nations can keep pace with the technological and economic explosion which we know will occur. And most important, if our abundance continues to grow more rapidly than in the Southern Hemisphere, as it appears bound to do, will the "haves" have the sense to share their bounty with the "have-nots" and to

19

establish relations between themselves which they would see followed by others, both rich and poor?

A world of instant communication and instant transportation and instant annihilation will bring men in this world too close together to rely for political stability on the nation-state system as we have known it and seen it work. If man can build a wheel to transport him, and then an automobile, and then an airplane, and then a rocket, surely he can evolve the human relations which will not make mobility a catalyst for conflict. If man can "progress" from the stick to the club, to the arrow, to the gun, to the bomb, and then to The Ultimate Bomb, surely he must find the ingenuity to create a political climate that allows people to live, rather than to die, together.

This is the great test of the next hundred years, indeed the next decade. As we are the beneficiaries of the earth's plenty and man's genius, so must we be the benefactors of political progress in the search for survival.

The major obstacle to this political progress—to the establishment of a model for relations among independent nations on the North American continent—is the failure of Americans to think of Canada as an independent country and to respect her independence. The fundamental principle of relations between states is a mutual respect for independence. Without it the fruitful partnership, on which the Merchant-Heeney Report and all other commentary on U.S.–Canadian relations seem based, is not possible. For partners are not partners if one takes the other for granted.

Why do Americans take Canada and Canadians for granted? There are at least three reasons: First, the basic national characteristics of the two countries are so similar. Second, U.S. education has not emphasized a Canadian national identity. Third, Canadians themselves are still engaged in defining that national identity.

In a very real sense Americans don't think of Canada as an independent country because Canadians are too close to us. They are of course close in geographic terms, but they are close in every other way—in culture, history, language, dress, food, sports, climate, politics, literature, religion.

If you name any other country in the world, an American will think of some major difference that divides its people from Americans. Ghana is a new country and principally black. Italy is a very old country and principally Catholic. Costa Ricans have a very small country, Russians are Communists, the British live on an island, the Japanese attacked us in a war, Bolivians speak Spanish, the Chinese eat rice, Moroccans are surrounded by sand, the French drink wine, the Indians wear saris, the Brazilians play soccer, and the Polish dance polkas.

But what of the Canadians? They have a Queen. They have a parliamentary form of government. Their major national sport is hockey. They have Frenchmen who speak French, and drink wine too. They're colder in the winter and cooler in the summer.

But none of these is a difference of substance or of note. They do not reflect basic national characteristics that are distinct from our own. When an American thinks of Canadians, he thinks essentially of other Americans. Puerto Rico to most Americans is more foreign than Canada. And the people from the Northern States see more differences between themselves and the Southern States than they do between themselves and Canada—in the South they talk "different," they fought a war against the North, and they eat such strange things as okra, hog jowls, and black-eyed peas.

This is not to say that there are not real differences between the United States and Canada—differences in history and politics and literature and perspective. It is to say, however, that by and large Americans are not aware of the differences, and as a result they are not really aware of Canada the independent nation, of Canada a country as politically distinct from the United States as Peru, Ceylon, or Romania.

Respect for the independence of a nation can only begin with awareness; and awareness of Canada in the United States can come only from Canada forcing us to take notice, and from our education. In those long years of American history when the United States was preoccupied with its own development, its schools taught very little about foreign lands—and then generally only about those old and distinguished European cultures from which we sprang. And Canada was not among them.

In the last generation, as the United States has begun to look outward upon the world, the most rapidly expanding area of education—primary, secondary, and university—has been in international relations. We have begun to study the history and the ways of peoples in far-distant and exotic lands—where we know there are great differences between us and we believe that greater understanding can lead to a safer world. We study the new, we study the different, we study where our foreign aid goes, we study where the crises emerge. And still Canada is not among them. In courses on comparative government, Canada is almost never included. Canadian history, politics, literature, art, and even geography are seldom learned or taught.

At the same time, Canada is precisely the country from which Americans seek the most—the natural result of geography. Only Canada can be the geographic buffer between the U.S. and the U.S.S.R. If we need water, we cannot get it from Tanzania, only from Canada. If we need a highway to connect our forty-eight contiguous states to our forty-ninth, we cannot go to Burma, only to Canada. Our electricity does not depend on the plugs being in the right sockets in Finland, only in Canada.

The basic long-range crisis in U.S.–Canadian affairs is that the U.S. people seek so much from a country whose independence they feel and respect so little. The solution is not to seek less, for there are immense benefits to both countries in each striving to meet the needs of the other. The solution is a greater respect for, understanding of, and awareness of the independence of Canada. That is why the White Paper on U.S.–Canadian affairs of September, 1965, published by eleven members of the U.S. House of Representatives and commonly referred to as the Tupper Report, placed so much stress on education in the United States—and that is why this book echoes that emphasis.

A beginning of education for awareness will come when Americans learn to appreciate the value to the United States of Canadian independence. It is one thing to learn the statistics and habits of a foreign country. It is another and more worthy goal of education to teach the contribution which Canadian experience can make to American life.

Two examples relevant to our professions of politics and political science may suffice. Few countries have had the opportunity to learn and build from the experience of another with similar history and similar culture. The experience of an independent Canada, if we will only look at her, can teach the United States two extraordinarily relevant lessons in political science that relate to two of our most cherished constitutional precepts—the division of powers, and the separation of powers.

Federalism in the United States is in grave danger. In part this is because the American states have preached more about preserving states' rights than they have practiced meeting states' responsibilities. They have failed to do what they have the capacity to do. But in many cases they simply do not even have the capacity to solve the problems that confront them. Despite the recent and valiant efforts of gifted governors in our most populous, industrial, and problem-ridden states, our system of federalism and our state governments are increasingly becoming anachronisms.

The major problem is a jurisdictional one. Population centers sprawl across state boundaries; the jurisdiction for problem-solving must be shared by two or more states. Competing programs are more common than coordinated ones. More common still is inaction—by one of the states responsible, or by them all. Recourse to the federal government for solution is inevitable and the role of the states diminishes proportionally.

When U.S. state boundaries were marked, each state contained completely the total population of cities within it. But as the population has grown, as mobility has increased, the urban sprawl has neither recognized nor respected state boundaries. The problem is particularly intense along the U.S. eastern coast—a megalopolis spread across nine states from Boston in the north to Washington in the south.

It is apparent to the political scientist that the diffusion of governmental power and authority, which is the justification and a reason for federation as a form of government, cannot be preserved in the United States without a fairly radical restructuring of our political map. Either we must create regional centers of government between the states and Washington or we must regroup our states into larger and more relevant political subdivisions.

A quick look at the map demonstrates in dramatic ways that the Canadian experience with federalism has been a different one. Recourse to Canadian history and political science texts confirms the judgment. The Canadian population will expand as ours has; but the Canadian provinces will be more capable of containing population sprawls and of retaining the capacity to meet their responsibilities. The average Canadian subdivision is four and one-half times the size of the average American state. We do not suggest that Canada deliberately created large provinces out of the wisdom to anticipate jurisdictional disputes as population and mobility expand. Nonetheless the Canadian experience offers some wise counsel for our future.

The same map of Canada shows another fact. Only once is a river used to separate two Canadian provinces. The fact is important, and if the United States ever does redraw state boundaries, it should take the knowledge into account. People do not found a city in the mountains, or on an artificial longitude or latitude. By and large, a city's location is determined by the ease of transportation to and from it—which means, or in the past has meant, that cities most often grow on the edge of rivers. If rivers are also state boundaries, an invitation to juris-

24

dictional disaster and the depletion of state authority is inevitable.

New York, New York, and Newark, New Jersey; Philadelphia, Pennsylvania, and Camden, New Jersey; St. Louis, Missouri, and East St. Louis, Illinois; Cincinnati, Ohio, and Covington, Kentucky; Kansas City, Missouri, and Kansas City, Kansas; Portland, Oregon, and Vancouver, Washington; and even Washington, D.C., itself. All these are multiple cities— multiple only because a state-boundary river runs through the middle of them. This fact complicates jurisdiction, limits the capacity of state government to meet major social and economic problems, expands the role of the federal government, and inevitably undermines the preservation of individual liberty through the concentration of authority, which it was the purpose of federalism to avoid.

Again it probably was not Canadian wisdom or foresight that led to the avoidance of rivers as provincial boundaries. If that wisdom had existed, the divided city of Ottawa/Hull would not today be presenting jurisdictional problems to the neighboring provinces of Ontario and Quebec. But whatever the cause, education in the Canadian experience could help provide American political scientists and politicians with a guide to a more relevant federal structure and map in their own country.

By the U.S. constitutional separation of powers, the executive, judicial, and legislative functions in the presidential system were to be co-equal. Today with the dominance of international affairs and the evolution of administrative machinery in Washington, the role of the Congress has proportionally diminished. It is no longer a source of initiative. The Congress can, of course, change and even reject legislation sponsored by the administration, but its powers to shape the nation and the world through creativity and innovation have by and large been absorbed by the executive office, the President, and his administration. This is not the result of one President or another. It is the result of a modern, urbanized, technologically advanced, and extremely complex society which has centralized in the figure of one man the power necessary to keep the government serving the people effectively.

Every man who has served in the Congress in the last decade has wondered how the role of Congress can be changed so that it can make a more effective contribution to government. Congress should not seek to take back from the President the power that has accrued to his office; it should seek the way by which the Congress can make more of a contribution than it has—hopefully in being able to advise and help the President to do a more responsible job. Perhaps the answer lies in giving to the Congress a greater responsibility in the development of long-range thinking and planning—in the holding of hearings and inquiries into long-range domestic and international problems. It is frequently in this area of long-range planning where the administration, charged with the responsibility of dealing with the day-to-day events, doesn't have ample opportunity to set the stage for new innovations in policy or to anticipate severe domestic or long-range crises and opportunities before they are obvious.

Education in the Canadian experience would provide the politician and the political scientist alike with a different model of government which nonetheless stems from a similar culture and history. The Canadian parliamentary system of operating government can provide ideas for the modernization and strengthening of government through a greater congressional participation in the formulation of policy.

Many Canadians would, no doubt, suggest that the Canadian Parliament is far more impotent than the American Congress. Many Canadian politicians and political scientists are disappointed at the contribution that its legislative branch is making to the affairs of government. But regardless of the innovations that might be appropriate to strengthen the hand of the Canadian Parliament, it is apparent that current Canadian parliamentary practice may give indications to the American Congress as to how better to integrate its activities with the executive branch and thereby to forge a channel for constructive creativity.

For example, would it be appropriate for the President's Cabinet either to be drawn from the Congress or to sit in the Congress? Such a radical innovation in U.S. political theory and practice might build the capacity of the Congress to influence the administration. More important, it might build the capacity of the administration to influence more directly the content of the Congressional effort to shape the future of American public affairs.

Canada should not be thought of as a laboratory experiment for U.S. reformers. But education in the Canadian experience would make the American people not simply more aware of Canada the country, but more aware as well of new means by which our own political, economic, and social systems can be made ever more effective.

The third reason why the people of the United States tend too often to take Canada and Canadians for granted is the fact that Canada in a very real sense is still engaged in a search for her own identity. Her historic ties with the British Commonwealth of Nations may today seem increasingly irrelevant. The constant shadow cast across her by a neighbor with incredible military and economic power makes the role she is to play on the world stage difficult to see with precision. Her historic ties to one hemisphere and her location in another point in opposite directions as she sets about to chart a course for the future.

This frustration and ambivalence results in policies not always clear, not always consistent. Her goals at times seem obscure. This is frequently said by foreigners about all nations, certainly including the United States. The most relevant fact about Canadian policy is that the Canadians themselves see the same inconsistencies and lack of clear purpose seen by others.

A growing American awareness of an independent Canada will depend in part upon the Canadian capacity to define its own identity—its goals, its purposes, the course it intends to follow—a national identity not dictated by the presence of American power but by the desire of Canadians to shape events to their own design.

The U.S. humorist Art Buchwald has counseled Canada on how to get noticed in the United States: burn the Stars and Stripes at Niagara Falls; demand that the U.S. give back the St. Lawrence Seaway; or build a Berlin-type wall along the boundary.[5] A more enduring course would be the pursuit of a foreign policy which is written in Ottawa rather than Washington.

The United States should not fear an independent Canadian foreign policy. On the contrary we should welcome it. The compatible culture, history, and values of the two nations must inevitably mean compatible goals in policy. The United States must learn to cherish the Canadian capacity to pursue an independent course toward those goals.

The united strength of the free-world nations arises not from automatic allegiance to the will of the most powerful. It stems from the mutual conclusion of independent states on the nature of the world they would will to the generations that follow—from the fact that their alliance represents a free choice. Whatever power the Communist world may claim, the very nature of the government they practice denies to them the strength inherent in independent peoples who, free to choose their own course, nonetheless choose to pursue a common dream.

Partnership between the United States and Canada cannot be possible or productive unless Canada has an independent foreign policy in which agreement with the U.S. is a matter of choice, not a matter of power.

Only an *independent* Canada, confident of her own identity and respected for it in the United States, can join with the United States to build a true model for relations between independent nations—to build on the virtues of nationalism and to minimize its vices.

In one sense it may be considered the highest of tributes when one people takes another for granted, for it means, in the case of the United States and Canada, that the American people know that the Canadians, above all peoples, share our hopes and our dreams, our fears and our concern for this ever more dangerous world. But successful international politics relies on the sensitivity of one country to the reactions of others to what it says and does and thinks. Sometimes people in the United States believe that Canadians are too suspicious of our motives—perhaps too cautious in jointly planning for the future out of fear that their national identity will be obscured.

Americans must come to know that if the Canadians are suspicious of our motives and cautious in accepting our policies, it is a reaction which comes from a long North American history when taking Canada for granted was far more than an insult. It was the threat of physical domination and annexation. In 1889, U.S. Secretary of State James G. Blaine said:

> Canada is like an apple on a tree just beyond our reach. We may strive to grasp it, but the bough recedes from our hold just in proportion to our effort to catch it. Let it alone and in due time it will fall into our hands.

Blaine was no better a prophet than John Quincy Adams when in 1823 he likened Cuba to the self-same apple, which, if "forcibly disjoined from its own unnatural connection with Spain, and incapable of self-support can gravitate only toward the North American Union." [6]

The point is not the wisdom of American secretaries of state. It is that throughout history the Americans have either sought to dominate Canada or have ignored her. Or worse, we have done both at the same time, as the Blaine quote suggests—and as some Canadians would charge we do today. The opportunity and the obligation of the future will leave little room for either course in the second hundred years.

Chapter II

Nationalism: Its Virtues, Its Vices

More than one hundred years ago, in 1865, an advertisement in the Brooklyn *Eagle* sought out volunteers with an adventuresome spirit to join an expedition which would either set out to conquer Mexico or set out to conquer Canada.[1]

A few years later the North American continent heard these strains of a marching song:

> We are the Fenian Brotherhood, skilled in the art of war,
> And we're going to fight for Ireland, the land we adore.
> Many battles we have won along with the boys in blue,
> And we'll go and capture Canada, for we've nothing else
>   to do.[2]

Students in the nuclear age may not understand that in an age of less vicious and total weapons, combat was a way of life for many men—and for many nations, war seemed a preoccupation. The year 1867 may have seen the birth of the Canadian Confederation, but it also was the approximate centennial of the emergence of the modern nation-state.

Nationalism as we know it today takes many forms—so many forms as to defy easy definition. A nation to some, as to Woodrow Wilson, can mean simply a people who share a common language. But the British Commonwealth is not a nation. To most it means those who share a common land. But the Jews were a nation for centuries without a land of their own. Nationalism is the bond among a people which often stems in part from a common language, a common territory,

30

and a common culture, but generally is inseparable from a common idea—the purpose of being, the mission of a nation, the reason for its existence. Nationalism is "identification with the life and aspirations of uncounted millions whom we shall never know, with a territory which we shall never visit in its entirety." [3] Nationalism requires "the fundamental condition of national consciousness, a common stock of memories of the past and of hopes for the future, which permeates the whole people and determines their mind and aspirations. . . ." [4]

In its contemporary form, the state as a nation was necessarily preceded by the rise of the modern state itself in the sixteenth and seventeenth centuries. But it descended also from the uniting power of religion—an idea which was as powerful a uniting force in ancient times as the devotion to the democratic ideal is today. Indeed it has been written:

> Abraham was not a man possessed with the vision of the one God, he was really the chieftain of the Bedouin tribe intent on endowing his horde with a national identity. Moses was not a man inspired by God in order to fulfill and reaffirm His covenant with Israel, he was really a national leader rising against colonial oppression. Muhammad may have been the seal of the Prophets, but even more important, he was the founder of the Arab nation.[5]

It was then the joining together of the fervor of an idea with the defined territory of a modern state which laid the basis for modern nationalism. But something else was needed. It was national participation in the affairs of the nation. It was people identified with the idea, with the territory, with the state. Thus, in a very real sense it was the American Revolution in 1776 which was the beginning of modern nationalism— and it was the French Revolution of 1789 which assured that the Old World, with its far-flung empires in every corner of the earth, would spread the organizing force of nationalism as Christianity, Judaism, and Mohammedanism had been spread before it.

31

Nationalism, the state of national consciousness, emerged not accidentally as merely one of three revolutions. National consciousness would have been impossible without the rise of democracy. And neither would have flourished without the industrial revolution—with its printing press, its quickened communication, and its capacity to provide prosperity for the masses.

Albert Einstein is reputed to have called nationalism "an infantile disease—the measles of mankind." But it is much too easy and superficial a judgment to condemn emotional, irrational, and reflexive nationalism as the source of war. The history of war and peace in Europe in the eighteenth, nineteenth, and early twentieth centuries is a grim one. None of the endless stream of European conflicts from the Napoleonic Wars to the Crimea, to Prussian imperialism, and up through World War I was devoid of belligerence that sprang from rampant national loyalties. But with nationalism in Europe came democracy and an organizing force for society through which the fruits of the industrial revolution could be spread among the people. For all its vices nineteenth-century nationalism had its virtues too.

And some, as Ramsay Muir in the midst of World War I, could see value even in the most extreme excesses of nationalistic fervor:

> . . . the nationalist movements of the nineteenth century [gave] a new stability and clearness to the political boundaries of Europe; for all experience shows that national boundaries, once established, are extraordinarily lasting. Thus the very wars which our sentimentalists bemoan as the evidence of an incurable European anarchy, have, in so far as they have defined the bounds of nation-states, brought nearer the possibility of an international system. For internationalism is dependent upon nationalism.[6]

Perhaps Muir thought as others did that World War I was "the war to end all wars." He may have anticipated too easy a demise for barbarian nationalism and too great a faith in the brotherhood of man within the "family of nations." In any event, the world's statesmen while striving for internationalism through creation of the League of Nations, subverted their own high purpose by setting in motion a harsh peace for the vanquished Germany which, far from pouring sand on the fires of German nationalism, only fanned their flames.

The internationalism preached at Versailles lasted for the United States only as long as the President was abroad. In Europe it lasted only as long as governments were not asked to sacrifice their national interest for the common good.

Only internationalism could have seen that the peace of Europe rested not in the isolation of Germany but in an international system that considered her interests among all others. Only internationalism, not nationalism, could have saved Europe from a Germany seeking revenge under the leadership of a madman.

Only internationalism, and devotion to the principles of collective security which placed the good of all men above national interest, could have saved Ethiopia from the total irrationality of a Mussolini.

Only internationalism and a commitment to more than mere national pride could have convinced a militant Japan that aggression, in Manchuria or elsewhere, was doomed to failure.

By the end of World War II, the lessons of World War I had been learned. The United States recognized its responsibilities and enthusiastically joined the United Nations. Neither Germany nor Japan was allowed to nurture its grievances in isolation. Each was tied closely to the Western nations that had conquered them so that any nationalistic excesses would be contained within a system of international commitment.

Finally, in postwar Europe began the extraordinary adventure in internationalism known as the unity of Europe. Never before in all human history had a continent of nations sought to build the political framework within which the vices of the nation-state system could be forever submerged in allegiance to a supranational entity.

33

Our contemporary preoccupation with President de Gaulle, and his curious blend of an exquisite vision of the future with a dubious concept of French grandeur from the past, should not be allowed to divert our attention from the exceptional achievements in international political and economic coopera- tion which the nations of Western Europe have made in the last decade. The Council of Europe, the Western European Union, the Coal and Steel Community, EURATOM, and the Common Market are spectacular achievements for nations that fifty years ago seemed always to be at one another's throat.

Nonetheless, De Gaulle's design for France should not di- vert our attention either from other remnants of European nationalism in the mid-1960's. We have welcomed, of course, the struggles of the East European satellites, particularly Hungary and Poland, to retain their national identity in the face of an imposed universalism from Moscow. Less welcome are the nationalistic clashes in Belgium between the Flemish and Walloons. Those of German stock in the Italian territory of South Tyrol are determined by one means or another to proclaim, maintain, and defend their national identity. The Spaniards, Basques, and Catalans remain at uneasy peace only through the imposed will of a dictator. The Greeks and the Turks in their homelands and in Cyprus are all too reminiscent of nineteenth-century Balkan history. And no one dare be complacent about the slow, but apparently determined, return of a flamboyant and belligerent German national consciousness.

What of the East? Communism, of course, does not spring from nationalism—on the contrary it is an idea largely imposed upon people. In the Soviet Union, in Eastern Europe, and in China it is imposed upon many different peoples and only over time through constant indoctrination can it become identified with a national consciousness. If it occurs, a sturdy Communist nationalism will be the product of the imposition of an idea. It will be the antithesis of Western nationalism, which emerged from the wellsprings of democracy. But it is proof again of the strength of an idea, no matter how wrong, that Communism in Russia has been the vehicle by which a kind of early nationalism has been built. It still remains to be seen whether the persistent ties of the historic nationality of peoples can be totally eradicated without the growth of democratic and free participation by the people in the affairs of the "nation."

Perhaps in the minds of most today, nationalism, in its most vibrant forms, is most evident in the southern half of the globe —in the struggles to define boundaries between newly independent states and in the competition for continental leadership in Latin America and Africa and Asia—so reminiscent of the European struggles of a century ago. Whatever its vices, let us not be blinded to the virtues of nationalism as a unifying and organizing force in the progress toward development of the new and independent nations. In pursuit of their lofty goal to achieve in one generation the material satisfactions which Western civilization has taken two centuries to acquire, the developing nations have employed, in many cases as their sole resource, the unifying features of a nationalism which can excite the people and incite them to work.

More often than not the nationalism of newly independent countries is expressed in negative terms. An external threat is either exaggerated or created so as to unite the people in a common cause. Once united they can then better strive for progress in domestic development programs. Thus India faces the threat of China; and Pakistan faces the threat of India; in Sukarno's heyday, Indonesia manufactured a war with Malaysia; Castro justifies every domestic program with reference to the need for national unity in the face of imminent U.S. invasion.

It is a practice not unknown to the United States and Canada. Neither must manufacture the malevolent competition of the Communist world, but the United States administrations, at least, have been prone to utilize an international crisis, in which popular concern reaches its height, to press for added defense appropriations from the Congress not entirely related to the needs of the immediate crisis.

This book was written because the world has been flung

into a new and crucial age. The geometric progression of science will no longer let us forgive the vices of nationalism simply because they are necessary if we are to take advantage of its virtues. It once was true that new strides forward in communication and mobility were necessary to progress from the fiefdom to a modern nation-state with a defined and broad territory. But mobility and communications have long since passed from the role of catalyst of the nation-state to the role of catalyst for international enmity. Knowledge of your fellow man or knowledge of your national neighbor does not ensure peace and harmony. In the context of the emotions of nationalism, knowledge of your neighbor may tend only to build a resentment or to underscore differences or to sow the seeds for inevitable conflict.

Perhaps once, as Ramsay Muir has suggested, the petty wars of nationalism served the purpose of defining national values so that internationalism could gain a foothold. But today, no matter how petty the causes for war between nations, the weapons for war between nations are surely not petty. Because knowledge of nuclear weapons exists, it borders on the inevitable that that knowledge will become simplified and spread among the people of the world. And after the knowledge the weapons themselves will follow.

We can try to promote international understanding and good will, by which communications and mobility will not be a catalyst for enmity. We can, and surely we must, take every step that is within our power to attempt to limit the proliferation of nuclear weapons among the nations and the peoples of this earth. We can and must seek disarmament. But we cannot expect that what never has been achieved in history can be achieved now simply because it must be so.

The traditional efforts are not enough. This is the obligation that rests on all nations and all national leaders—to create a new world in which the vices and excesses and emotions of nationalism can be stripped away and the virtues of nationalism retained. As an organizing force, as a source of national pride and national work, as a means of giving identity to a

36

people, nationalism, like the great religions before it, can be a force for great good. On these virtues, this world must find the way to build political institutions which will turn growing international contact from a precursor of conflict to a prelude for progress.

This obligation rests most heavily on the two giant states on the North American continent. For all their progress since the end of World War II, the nations of Western Europe are beset by a seemingly endless stream of persistent obstructions to the growth of genuine international unity—obstructions inherent in the history of modern Europe so productive of mistrust, suspicion, and occasional vengeance.

By our history, by our abundance, by our geographic isolation the future places this challenge uniquely at our feet—to create on the North American continent a model of relations between independent states—to build here an example of international relations which we would have all men and all nations follow.

Thomas Huxley once wrote: "Size is not grandeur, and territory does not make a nation." [7] What then if not size, has made our nations? What is the history of nationalism on the North American continent?

Hans Kohn, the leading Western scholar on the subject of nationalism, has said that:

North America actually falls as short of being united as Europe does. The distrust of the United States felt in Canada and Mexico is comparable to that felt in many European countries toward France or Germany, toward their actual or possible hegemonial aspirations. [8]

The sources and sense of nationalism in the United States and Canada differ broadly between the two countries. United States nationalism has been shaped predominantly by one event and one idea—the American Revolution of 1776 and man's right to be free. The rebels in the thirteen colonies did, after all, share the language, the traditions, the culture, the

37

literature, and the history of those against whom they rebelled. In fact, the Revolution, in a very real sense, was undertaken in the name of British constitutionalism, which had been subverted by George III. The common bond among the colonies at the outset of the Revolution was hardly sufficient to hold promise for the birth of a new nation.

But the American Revolution forged unity around an idea. The break from the mother country was clean, swift, and complete. From that moment on, the United States had a national consciousness inseparable from a mission—a mission ofttimes poorly conceived and inappropriately pursued, but a mission that became the driving force for an entire nation. As Kohn has said: "Though the feeling of responsibility to and for mankind was sometimes submerged in the naive egotism of a self-righteous isolationism, it was always present." [9]

The mission was present when the spirit of the new nation was intent upon taming the West. And when taming the West proved insufficient to satisfy the pioneer spirit, American nationalism and its mission became the justification for the jingoism of the Mexican and Spanish-American Wars.

It was, of course, throughout this same period, the last sixty years of the nineteenth century, that many misinterpreted the mission to dictate the inevitable annexation of Canada. The urge for annexation in the United States can be exaggerated, however. In a practical sense, despite the fervent preachings of self-appointed prophets, the forceful annexation of Canada was not considered seriously by thoughtful men after the War Hawks in the War of 1812 were thwarted. From that date, talk of annexation was really limited to border areas and individual spokesmen seeking attention more than war. This does not mean that the claims were not heard. Consider, for example, the 1850 resolution of the New York Legislature, "that the annexation of Canada, and other provinces of Great Britain in North America . . . is an object of incalculable importance to the people of the United States." [10]

Twentieth-century U.S. nationalism has seemed less jingoistic, less belligerent. To some, of course, it may appear that

38

the military nationalism of the nineteenth century has merely been replaced by an economic nationalism of the twentieth. At both ends of the Western Hemisphere, American economic intervention and domination have been both charged and feared.

But essentially, the twentieth century has seen the American sense of mission translated into a more rational and more idealistic promotion of the universal idea of the American Revolution—the right of man to be free.

The United States entered World War I "to make the world safe for democracy." We were not so uniformly convinced of the universality of our idea that we would agree to our President's negotiation of the internationalist League of Nations. But we had come out of our hemisphere—and we were to come out again twenty years later, and this time to stay. We promoted and gave a home to the United Nations. And we have sought to give it real meaning by defining its role in international crises—and by not imposing upon it obligations in great-power disputes that it could not resolve.

Postwar United States has committed herself to the world and to wage its battles in its far corners. Thus Berlin and Beirut, Seoul and Saigon are proof that, whatever the nobility of our mission, we have concluded that it cannot be served by ignoring the fate of others.

Any American would reluctantly have to admit that the strains of jingo nationalism, of witch-hunt nationalism, have not completely vanished from the scene in the United States. Surely the spectacle of McCarthyism, the overtones of the 1964 presidential campaign, and upon occasion, the American overreaction to the Communist menace, all clearly recall the vibrant if reckless national spirit of a less dangerous age.

So too does the cavalier U.S. attitude toward Canada. We have not fully understood that those who are our neighbors, and we assume will always be our friends, can resent domination over and intrusion in their affairs only for so long without sacrificing friendship in order to give vent to their own national aspirations and frustration.

U.S. dominance in U.S.–Canadian relations is in part made possible by the fact that Canada has not yet fully established the course of her own national aspirations. Until she does so, until her national identity is recognized and embraced by her own people, it is unlikely that it can have continuing impact elsewhere.

What is the source of the apparent Canadian bewilderment over its own national identity? Just as the dominant fact in United States history was its clean, effective, and total break with Great Britain through a revolution which united its people, surely the dominant fact of Canadian history is that it did not break away from the Old World in clean and bold strokes. A name like "British Maine" would seem as uncomfortable in the U.S. as "British Columbia" seems comfortable in Canada. In 1967 the Canadians will celebrate not the centennial of their revolution, not even the centennial of their full independence, but the centennial of their Confederation. Their independence was granted peacefully and gradually, without great bloodshed and without the opportunity or necessity to forge a national consciousness. Recognition of this fact is not to worship bloodshed, but to understand a source of Canadian indecision.

It is worth while to recall that during the American Revolution, the loyalists shared a common descent, common language, common traditions, and common territory with the rebels but were irrevocably separated from them by an idea. When the loyalists left, most of them went to Canada. On the other hand, when England acquired Canada in 1763 most French-Canadians "though entirely different in descent, language, traditions, and territory, were not forced to emigrate; and they did not choose to do so, but remained unhampered under the liberty and tolerance of the British Empire."[11]

The point is not the glories of the British Empire, but the absence of a national identity in Canada. This was as true of the French colonists as of the British. Van Tyne, in writing of the French-Canadians who supported the U.S. rebellion in 1776, pointed out that whereas they used to be the subjects of

France, "they were since so to England, they would be the same to the Emperor of Morocco." [12] Nationalism in Canada at the time of the American Revolution was unknown.

In their own fight against the West, in the need for protection in the face of the nineteenth-century U.S. zeal for annexation, and even today in the defense of their economy from U.S. domination, the Canadians have created a national entity and have developed a nationalism of their own. But it surely is not imbued with the missionary zeal that accompanied American history. For Canada was not a nation born with bloodshed in the wake of an idea—a nation unique in its own mind.

In a very real sense, the Canadian identity in international relations has been inseparable from the British Commonwealth of Nations—and Canadian foreign policy has often seemed to reflect more its membership in the Commonwealth than its own national aspirations. It does not minimize the Canadian contribution in World War I or in World War II to appreciate that in both cases the decision was less one of national determination than it was one of commitment to the motherland. Lest this be confused with criticism, it should be admitted that the United States made a very late entry into World War I and entered World War II only when it had no choice to avoid it.

In Korea, another interesting comparison can be made. The American national consciousness, combined with the responsibilities of leadership and a sense of mission to preserve and promote the idea of man's right to be free, led to a quick national decision to defend the territory of a nation far away, challenged by an alien and contradictory idea. Again the Canadian contribution was real and significant, but its decision for involvement was more determined by the decision of the United Nations than it was by a national commitment or a national consciousness that made it clear that this fight was Canada's fight too.

The contributions that Canada has made to the development of the United Nations as an effective international body for collective security and the resolution of conflict underscore

41

again the thesis that Canada's national identity, national purpose, and nationhood have yet to be made firm.

And final evidence of the same fact is the French–Canadian separatist movement. While it never at any stage has achieved monumental proportions even among the French–Canadian community, it nonetheless attests to the absence of a unifying idea to accompany Canadian nationhood, through which diverse elements can be subsumed in the pursuit of an objective which is held by all.

The Canadian search for identity—for a national consciousness in support of a national purpose—is of course complicated by the continuing decline of the British Commonwealth of Nations as a rational and effective international group for the pursuit of national goals, and by the ever present reality of the power of Canada's only neighbor. Membership in the Commonwealth of Nations complicates the Canadian search for identity because it teaches loyalties and habits which may have little in common with those that a well-defined Canadian nationalism might encourage. And a search for national purpose in the shadow of the immense military, economic, and idealistic power of a neighbor is surely not easy. But nations, unlike scholars, cannot retreat from reality simply because they are not yet ready for a decision. Canada's foreign policy must continue even as the secrets of her national purpose are probed.

This history of nationalism would suggest that the Canadian search for a unifying idea into which to channel the energies of its nation would ordinarily be expected to result in the emergence of a negative response to the presence of a powerful United States on its border. Such are the vices of nationalism that the dominant theme of the identity for which Canada seeks may in fact become anti-Americanism.

Thus the challenges to our two countries are extraordinary. In an age when the excesses of nationalism can combine with the weapons of annihilation to tear our earth apart, we have an obligation on the North American continent to build the institutions of political and economic relations which can serve as a model for the relations between independent states everywhere. It is impossible unless Canada pursues its search for national identity in the recognition that anti-Americanism is surely no more progressive a concept than the unifying features of Old World nations or of newly independent nations—unity through the exaggeration of or preoccupation with an external threat. The purpose of Canadian nationhood must surely be more than that.

And an exemplary North American model of international relations is impossible unless the United States on its part understands that international cooperation or partnership is progressive only when each partner has a full measure of respect for the independence and nationhood of the other. To paraphrase Ramsay Muir, we must have the wisdom to learn that only countries confident in their national purpose and their power to affect events can contribute to the building of a more rational international order. For "internationalism is dependent upon nationalism."

The words of George Gissing may carry the most important lesson of all: "It is because nations tend to stupidity and baseness that mankind moves so slowly; it is because individuals have a capacity for better things that it moves at all." [13] The North American challenge rests with both the Canadian and American peoples—perhaps more than with their governments. A progressive unifying idea cannot be imposed upon but springs from a people. If the Canadian people abdicate this responsibility, the unifying theme may be an entirely regressive anti-Americanism imposed by the reality of American power.

The people of the United States, in their turn, must learn that a mission is not always best pursued through the zeal of a missionary. The democratic ideal can be thwarted, rather than served, by policies inattentive to the aspirations of others. Now that the United States has become aware of the world, it is incumbent on Americans to become more aware of the peoples who live in it.

Chapter III

Foreign Policy: Power and Obligations

The Canadian search for a national role in international affairs inevitably takes place in the shadow cast by the power of her neighbor. In every area of public concern it is impossible for Canada to ignore or to wish away United States power. In foreign policy, perhaps above all spheres, the unequal capacity to shape events is most obvious—and most disturbing to Canadians.

The articulate and provocative foreign-policy critic at the University of Toronto, Professor James Eayrs, has dwelt at length on "the politics of disparate power"—on the course available to Canadian foreign policy in the face of overwhelming military and economic power at her border. The Eayrs three-tiered thesis is simple enough: First, the most remarkable feature of U.S.–Canadian relations is the use of restraint by the United States despite its power to dictate Canadian foreign policy. Second, the reason the United States exercises such great restraint in its relations with Canada is that it knows that it need not use its power or threaten to use its power to achieve its will—that merely the existence of power is sufficient to insure Canadian support of U.S. foreign policy. Third, the underlying feature of all Canadian foreign policy is that seldom, if ever, is Ottawa willing to take any decision that it suspects may aggravate Washington.[1]

Eayrs' historical conclusions are all too accurate. The Canadian dilemma is how to find a uniquely Canadian role in international relations while at the same time keeping not one but both eyes fixed firmly on Washington and its power.

The Merchant–Heeney Report of June 1965 demonstrated the dilemma. There are no two more skilled or experienced diplomats in North American relations than Livingston Merchant and A. D. P. Heeney. Charged with the responsibility of producing a semi-official bilateral report on the principles which should guide relations between the two countries, their product was inevitably hampered by the stilted language of diplomacy, the need for good manners, and the undoubted desire of their respective government leaders not to rock the boat. What their report had to say about foreign policy upset some Canadians but its ripples did not rock the boat.

In the conduct and development of their unique bilateral relationship, however, the two countries must have regard for the wider responsibilities and interests of each in the world and their obligations under various treaties and other arrangements to which each is a party.

This principle has a particular bearing upon our affairs in relation to the heavy responsibilities borne by the United States, generally as the leader of the free world and specifically under its network of mutual defense treaties around the globe. It is important and reasonable that Canadian authorities should have careful regard for the United States Government's position in this world context and, in the absence of special Canadian interests or obligations, avoid, so far as possible, public disagreement especially upon critical issues. This is not to say that the Canadian Government should automatically and uniformly concur in foreign policy decisions taken by the United States Government. Different estimates of efficacy and appropriateness or degree of risk generate honest differences of opinion among the closest allies. The Canadian government cannot renounce its right to independent judgment and decision in the "vast external realm." On its part Canada has special relations and obligations, some of which the United States does not share but of which it should take account, in particular with Great Britain and the other states of the Commonwealth, with France, and with certain other nations.

It is in the abiding interest of both countries that, wherever possible, divergent views between the two governments should be expressed and if possible resolved in private, through diplomatic channels. Only a firm mutual resolve and the necessary practical arrangements to keep the totality of the relationships in good and friendly working order can enable our countries to avoid needless frictions and minimize the consequences of disagreement.[2]

Thus the bilateral position is that Canada has every right to arrive at "different estimates of efficacy and appropriateness"; Canada has a "right to independent judgment and decision"; that Canada need not "automatically and uniformly concur" in U.S. policy; *but* that Canada must make every effort to keep quiet about any significant disagreement.

If this means that each ally should attempt to consult on all policy differences with the leader of the alliance, if it means that in times of immediate crisis unresolved differences (even after consultation) should preferably not be aired, and if it means that every government has the responsibility in formulating its own foreign policy to take into consideration the interest of its allies, we heartily concur. But if it means that Canada is to defer to U.S. leadership in all its interests that are not uniquely Canadian, we must respectfully disagree.

There are, of course, distinct responsibilities that the United States must face as the leader of the free association of free-world nations. Though Canada does not share them, she can hardly be unaware of them. But Canada's status as a "middle" power imposes upon her distinct obligations which the United States does not share—and these, by and large, the United States Government has failed to recognize. It is in these middle-power responsibilities that the Canadian Government has the opportunity to make its greatest contribution toward world peace, in which Canada may most satisfactorily define her national identity, and in which a Canadian foreign policy independent from United States dictation may be invaluable to both countries.

The United States did not seek its role as leader of the free-world nations. Its history, its geography, and above all its economic and military power imposed the responsibilities of leadership upon her. The responsibilities of the leader are the same, however, whether leadership is the product of choice or chance. Simply stated they are four: the responsibility to assure that the free association of free-world nations has sufficient power for defense and deterrence; the responsibility to assure that that power is used when necessary to preserve world peace; the responsibility to promote the independence of nations that desire to be free; and the responsibility to seek a consensus foreign policy among all nations of the free association which it leads.

Acceptance of the awesome responsibility to assure that the free world has sufficient military power for defense and deterrence is why the United States remains the free-world leader even if at times its foreign policies seem less progressive or relevant than those promoted by others. Almost without exception, the United States Government and people have been willing since the end of World War II to spare no funds to provide adequate nuclear and conventional forces to deter any Communist aggression—and to defend against Communist aggression if deterrence fails.

Despite extraordinary pressures in Western Europe to establish a separate identity from the United States, the nations of Western Europe will continue to be primarily influenced by the course of American foreign policy. No less a national leader than Charles de Gaulle, seeking the grandeur that his France once knew, surely measures each step of national policy against what he believes to be the limit of U.S. exasperation. De Gaulle must know that a France with an independent foreign policy— or a Europe "independent" of the United States—is possible only because by culture, by history, and by devotion to the democratic ideal the U.S. umbrella of power will remain the basic physical source of European security.

While no one should deny the psychological comfort that an independent nuclear capacity may give a nation *or* the psychological discomfort which any independent nuclear capacity may give to its potential target, it is nonetheless true that the French nuclear force is not now, nor is it likely to become, the major deterrent to the Soviet Union or to Soviet designs on Western Europe. The U.S. nuclear force is and will remain the preoccupation of any would-be aggressor against Western Europe.

However any nation or any leader may bemoan alleged shortcomings in American foreign policy, no one should argue that it has failed to meet its responsibilities of leadership—to provide sufficient power to deter and defend against major aggression faced by free-world nations. In the exercise of this first responsibility the United States has, of course, created obstacles for the exercise of its other responsibilities of leadership. When a nation expands its power it inevitably causes a psychological reaction within those nations with whom it must deal. Though it may not use its power, no one is unaware that the power exists—and this fact alone may raise in the minds of foreign peoples a distaste for the United States. And when the power is nuclear power and the foreign people a neighbor, the psychological reactions may be even more intense. The United States can act to minimize ill will, it can seek to understand the reactions to its power, it can be sensitive to the fears and concerns of others, but it cannot ignore the unique responsibility that leadership has imposed.

The second responsibility of free-world leadership—to use power when necessary to preserve world peace—has caused even greater pain in the United States. President Truman was said to keep on his wall a small plaque which read: "The buck stops here." In the arena of international politics, the buck stops with the United States. When aggression against the free

48

world occurs, theoretically the responsibility to respond falls equally on the shoulders of all free men. But in practice the responsibility of response falls disproportionately upon the United States.

This is not merely a function of its power. It is even more a result of the fact that leadership requires action. Other nations may debate the right course to follow. Other nations may moralize. Other nations may rationalize that the challenge is not theirs to meet. All of them can take comfort that the world does not look to them for action. They can afford to look elsewhere—to the leader.

The United States does not have the luxury of waiting for others to act. As with the leader of any group, whether it be the PTA or the free association of free-world nations, the United States must confront the harsh probability that, if it does not act, no one will.

Thus while others questioned our policies and debated their own, the responsibilities imposed upon the United States left it no choice but to act decisively in Iran, in the Berlin blockade, in Lebanon, in Cuba, in the Dominican Republic, in Korea, and in Viet Nam.

We do not suggest that the United States policy in each of these cases was undoubtedly wise or undebatably correct. Our point is another one altogether—that the responsibilities of leadership do not afford the United States time for reflection— or even time to be absolutely confident of the justice of its course. Other nations may wait to see what the United States does. The United States can wait for no one. The buck stops here.

The third responsibility of free-world leadership is to try to build the strength of the free and non-Communist world to preserve or promote the stability and independence of nations that are or would be free. As with the exercise of military power, the responsibility to use economic power to preserve the free world intact as a practical matter rests primarily with the United States. Ours is, of course, the nation that can most

49

afford a foreign-aid program, but the responsibility of development aid lies with the United States not simply because of its fantastic prosperity and abundance. This too, in large part, is the result of the fact that if the United States does not act, which nation shall?

It is important, upon occasion, for the Americans, their neighbors, their friends, and their foes to realize just how great an economic contribution the United States makes to the stability of the free world. Through the Marshall Plan, the bilateral foreign-aid programs, multilateral development agencies, the financing of the United Nations, an unparalleled balance of payments deficit which allows the aid programs to be funded, and untold numbers of private American contributions to programs abroad, the United States people have permitted their money to be used in what must be termed the most generous act of one people toward others in all human history. And the generosity is all the more notable because the American people receive very little in return—either in the form of visible results or even in the form of visible gratitude.

Of course, the richest people on earth should foot more of the bill than anybody else. Obviously we would welcome all the help that we can get. But the United States cannot escape the reality that it must continue to act even if no other nation does.

The final responsibility of leadership is to seek to define policies that others will follow. The basic strength of the free association of free-world nations is the free choice each of them makes to participate in the common effort. As the United States has become painfully aware, the leader of the free-world association cannot dictate policy to its followers. It must try and try and try again to reach a consensus, to forge among the free-world nations a common approach to the common problems which they face. When it speaks, it speaks not just as another nation of the world but as a leader of the free-world coalition—and thus innovation or experimentation in policy is difficult if not impossible.

Other nations can afford to be wrong, but not the free-world leader. Other nations can test out a thesis before adopting it as final policy to be followed, but not the United States, not the leader. Other nations can boldly set out on an isolated policy adventure without necessarily affecting all mankind or undermining the cohesion of the Western world—but not the leader, not the United States.

This requirement of leadership is, of course, at direct odds with the first three. In the maintenance of military power, in the use of military power, in the extension of economic assistance, the United States must act even if it must act alone. These responsibilities might be interpreted as leadership by example, but the fourth responsibility is that leadership must be exercised by consensus. For each of the crises in which the United States must act alone, there are a hundred areas in which unilateral U.S. action would be disastrous. When the United States bypasses its allies to negotiate with the Soviet Union, it sets an unfortunate example which all the other free-world nations then feel free to follow. When it tries to dictate a course for its Western European allies, it undermines their confidence and North Atlantic cohesion. When it pursues a narrow definition of its own national interest at the United Nations, it dramatically reduces its capacity to influence others to follow its leadership.

In short the United States must, in the most difficult of circumstances, act alone; in all other circumstances the United States must never act alone. No other nation can make that statement.

These are the foreign-policy obligations of the United States, of which the Merchant-Heeney Report spoke. What are the foreign-policy obligations of Canada, of which the Merchant-Heeney Report did not speak?

Canada, as a "middle" power in the free association of free-world nations, unencumbered by the limitations imposed by leadership, has the opportunity, and in our view the obligation, to conduct a different kind of policy. We are confident that the cultural, historical, and political compatibility of the United States and Canada will never permit substantive disparity in the foreign-policy goals of the two nations—despite substantive disparity between the power of the two nations, and despite an increasingly flexible Canadian foreign policy. The responsibilities of a "middle" power in foreign policy include: innovation; mediation; experimentation; and the exercise of international influence in spheres unavailable to those charged with leadership.

In each of these four areas, an independent foreign policy conducted within the framework of the free association of free-world nations can greatly strengthen the capacity of the entire free-world coalition to achieve its common goals. Canadian foreign policy has in the past made immense contributions toward objectives which it shares with the United States. But at times Americans tend only to see that the Canadian policy is different—not that it may be constructive nor that it may be beneficial to long-range U.S. interests as well.

The middle power has the capacity to *innovate,* to be creative in the area of foreign affairs. Canada shares this opportunity with others and to a limited extent has exercised it. In April 1965, Prime Minister Lester Pearson on a visit to the United States suggested that a pause in the American bombing of North Vietnamese targets might permit the Communist government in Hanoi, without losing face, to take an initiative of its own to bring about meaningful negotiations and an end to the Southeast Asian conflict. The following month a short-term pause in the bombing was tried. In December 1965 and January 1966, a complete interruption of American bombing in North Viet Nam was extended over a thirty-seven-day period. While neither of these efforts to provide the Communists with an opportunity to move closer toward peace was successful, each was well worth trying. At times those involved intimately in an international crisis may be too close to retain a thoroughly reasonable perspective. The ideas and innovation of others, if properly appreciated by those who lead, can be an extraordinary contribution to the keeping of the peace.

In another area Canadian innovation has not received the same attention from the United States administration. Perhaps no country is a greater champion of the United Nations, its purposes, and its programs than is Canada. Largely at Canadian initiative, and through Canadian example, many of the middle powers at the U.N. have now earmarked specific military forces for potential use by the world organization in peacekeeping operations. These stand-by units are available for call by the Secretary General when he is given authority to forge a peacekeeping unit and send it to a crisis spot.

For obvious reasons, stand-by units of national forces for U.N. peacekeeping operations are most valuable from the small and middle powers. Great-power combat forces may raise so many fears that a small crisis may develop into a great power conflict that their use in U.N. peacekeeping has been limited. Nonetheless, United States transport and logistic support of the U.N. operations in the Congo and the actual use of British forces in the U.N. peacekeeping effort in Cyprus have shown that even the great powers may be called upon to play a vital role in U.N. peacekeeping operations.

The United States, following Canadian example and innovation, should establish its own one-thousand-man unit of non-combat forces to be on call to the Secretary General for use in peacekeeping emergencies. This one-thousand-man force could consist of transport experts, linguistic experts, supply and quartermaster personnel, medical and health service personnel, communications engineers, and other personnel designed to support a U.N. operation without necessarily participating directly in policing or combat functions. The unit could be permanently headquartered at a base in the United States, trained in language and basic principles of international relations, equipped with appropriate gear for sudden assignment anywhere in the world, and drawn from volunteers in the existing armed forces.

Such a unit, as recommended by a group of Republican members of the House of Representatives, might be called the FIRST Brigade of the United States Armed Forces (Forces for International Relief on STand-by).

The *Toronto Daily Star,* in an editorial on March 16, 1966, commented on the need in Canada for a parliamentary equivalent to the U.S. Senate Committee on Foreign Relations. One of the functions of the U.S. Congress, in our view, is to provide a forum for new ideas in foreign policy, to inject creativity and innovation into foreign-policy consideration, and to consider alternative courses of policy in the areas of long-range United States concern.

Whatever the Canadian need for a counterpart to the Senate Committee, it is important to appreciate how much greater an impact can be made on U.S. foreign policy if the creativity and innovation stems not merely from the American Congress but from American allies in the coalition of free-world nations. When Canada restrains new ideas in policy for fear of the degree of acceptance they will receive in Washington, it disserves that coalition of nations to which both it and the United States belong. When the United States either ignores the new ideas of others or acts to restrain others from innovation in policy, it disserves the coalition as well.

It is possible, but difficult, for the leader to innovate; it is impossible for the leader to mediate—at least in any dispute that involves the great powers. A mediator, by definition, cannot be an active participant—and a leader of the free association of free-world nations has a responsibility to be a participant in any challenge which confronts the free world. Canada, largely through its participation in U.N. peacekeeping operations, has served a vital postwar role as a mediator in international crises. Its troops have gone with the U.N. wherever the U.N. has gone—to Cyprus, to the Congo, to Korea, to Kashmir, to Palestine, to Gaza-Sinai, to Lebanon, to West New Guinea, and to Yemen. Its military and political leaders have always been viewed as appropriate members for U.N. efforts to contribute a third and impartial voice to the consideration of international problems.

Paramount in this role today is the Canadian membership on the International Control Commission (ICC) in Viet Nam. While some Americans may be quick to criticize Canada and all other nations who do not have combat troops fighting at our side in Viet Nam, it is reassuring to others to know that precisely because Canadians are not fighting in the war their ICC membership provides the free world with a continual opportunity to work quietly and effectively for a peaceful settlement.

In April 1966, the Honorable Paul Martin, Canadian Secretary of State for External Affairs, described the mediating role which he hoped the ICC members could play:

> What we have in mind is something . . . modest and informal. It is really in the nature of a good-offices assignment which would be undertaken, not necessarily by the Commission as such but by the three Commission powers acting as sovereign nations which have been associated with the Viet Nam problem for the past 11 years or so and which have established a fair record of co-operation between them. It is our view that their knowledge and experience of the Viet Nam problem and the ready access they command to all the interested parties would make the Commission powers a particularly suitable group to carry forward the search for peace in Viet Nam, which is our common objective . . .[3]

A negotiated solution to Viet Nam will come, of course, only when both sides are willing to negotiate. But equally necessary is some channel through which each of them can communicate to the other their sincerity about negotiations and the conditions under which negotiations can take place. This will not happen through the public-relations world of the press conference. It will happen in the halls of diplomacy where the International Control Commission and Canada stand ready to be the catalyst for peace. Power and the will to use it may be the best guarantors of peace in an imperfect world, but the diplomats of peace are most often those, not with the power to make war, but with the posture to serve a peaceful future.

The United States cannot *experiment* in foreign policy—its power is so great and the stakes are so high that when it is not right the first time, it may not have a second time. In a real sense it must rely on others to test new adventures in policy and to open the channels for change. Canada as a middle power has an opportunity, and an obligation, when consistent with its national interest, to experiment in world affairs. No doubt this means upon occasion that it will embark upon courses that the United States disfavors and it may well run the risk of some alienation. But in the long run, United States policy changes most often follow the experiments of others who have had the foresight and capacity to test for change.

The United States now seems ready to debate with itself new efforts to normalize some areas of its relations with Communist China. In time this may mean the consideration of trade with Communist China. When that debate comes, the United States will no doubt wish to look at the experience of Canada and the success of her trade practices with the Communist world. The experience of others might enable the United States to decide whether to follow a similar course. For all that the United States may complain today about Canadian trade policies with the Communist world, they nonetheless may help provide the free world sufficient experience to justify a change in free-world policies.

We do not suggest that Canada experiment in foreign policy merely to test the water before the United States takes a plunge. Nonetheless, from the American point of view, it would be invaluable if allied experience existed on which to judge the value of a possible change in the direction of U.S. policy.

Americans are not excepted from the rule that all peoples believe that foreign-policy changes are premature if they themselves are not prepared to make them. We hope, however, that our nation is not so proud as to forget that it was not the first North American nation to come to the defense of Europe in either World War I or World War II. Indeed, in the 1941 words of Mackenzie King:

Canada's example, as a nation of the new world, actively participating to the utmost limit in the present struggle, has also had its influence in arousing the people of the United States to their present realization that freedom itself is at stake in this war.[4]

Finally, a middle power in international affairs may have a capacity to *influence* the course which others would follow quite unrelated to the coercive power it may be able to bring to bear. Frequently, as in Viet Nam, neither the United States people nor even all the members of their government are fully convinced that U.S. policy is right. It is the curse of leadership that one must upon occasion act before he has made a final and irrevocable decision on the justice of the case.

States with lesser responsibilities seldom confront this predicament. They can and most often do take the time to assure themselves that their course is correct, that their choice is clear, that their policy is right. Their decision on the course and policy to follow has not been dictated either by the circumstances of leadership or by the power of others. This capacity for free choice, combined with the absence of overwhelming power, often gives them an opportunity to influence the choice of others through the use of reason and logic. If this seems an unreal value in the harsh world of international relations, it is only because all men today tend to think only of the influence wielded through degrees of coercion. Physical power may convince a nation to follow a particular course, but it seldom can convince a nation of the justice of that course.

The great powers simply have too much power to be influential through logic. But those whose choice is based on reason, and who do not have the power to coerce, may be more capable of persuading the nations of the world to join freely in a vital cause.

These differences in the responsibilities of great and middle powers, of the United States and Canada, have been drawn to emphasize one essential fact: If Canadian foreign policy is written in Washington, it cannot serve Canadian interests ideally, or American interests either. We presume that an anti-American foreign policy in Canada is as inconceivable as an anti-Canadian foreign policy is in the United States. But a Canadian government free to innovate, free to mediate, free to experiment, free to influence the choice of others, not only can serve the Canadian national interest by helping to define the elusive identity which the nation seeks, but it can serve American interests as well.

Traditional commentary on foreign policy between the United States and Canada seems inevitably to concentrate on one feature—the joint consultation on common foreign-policy matters. Up to this point, that subject has been avoided here primarily to emphasize the extraordinarily different obligations which the power differences between the two countries impose upon them in international relations. Nonetheless, it is a fact that allies, and surely allied neighbors, can best serve their individual and common goals by full consultation on policy.

Unfortunately, to many Americans and increasingly to many in the North Atlantic Community, the word "consultation," when applied to foreign-policy discussions with the United States, has become synonymous with the dictation of an American blueprint to the allies. It should mean the sharing of information and the attempt to reach a common policy, undertaken with the awareness that at times divergent policies designed to pursue common goals may be the best means of achieving those goals.

The sharing of information and the joint consultation on foreign policy should be more standardized in U.S.–Canadian relations. As will be discussed later, the International Joint Commission, so marvelous a vehicle for the sharing of technical information and knowledge in less controversial areas, might well become the focal point for a continuous dialogue on foreign policy between the two countries. The process should not be practiced only when one country becomes conscience-stricken over its obligations toward the other. It should be a continual process from which can grow a greater understanding between the two governments and a greater understanding by each of the interests and intentions of the other.

Professor Eayrs, in a speech before the Michigan State University Inter-Collegiate Conference on U.S.–Canadian Affairs in April 1966, spoke of the "reckless generosity" of the White Paper on U.S.–Canadian Relations issued in the previous September and previously mentioned. That is a view fully consistent with the perspective from which he has analyzed the history of U.S.–Canadian affairs. Power relationships and balance of power politics which he assumes have dictated Canadian foreign policy toward the United States and United States reactions to Canada are surely a reality in our world.

We would be so bold as to suggest, however, that the true uniqueness of the U.S.–Canadian relations is that despite the disparity of power between the two countries the power relationship is less important than between almost any other two nations in the world. A country with great power can afford to be sensitive to another country without it. We assume that if this world is to survive it must find a better organizing force than the sheer escalation of national power in order to balance one nation against the next. It needs a new model of relations, and we assume that our common continent can provide it. The world—this nuclear world—can no longer afford to play the game of power politics among all the more than one hundred nations.

The dominant fact of the North American past is not the restraint which the United States has exercised in the use of its power toward Canada. The dominant fact is that relations between the two countries would make anything but restraint in the use of power unthinkable. This is why the opportunity exists for Canada and the United States to chart a new course in international behavior. This is why their obligation is so great.

The beginnings will be found in a greater definition of Canadian identity and a greater awareness of it in the United States. One such beginning can be found in a new appreciation in both countries of the value of a Canadian foreign policy written in Ottawa, not Washington.

59

Chapter IV

Defense: Is There Any Choice?

Nothing compromises the Canadian search for a national identity more severely than the problems of defense in the nuclear age.

When wars were fought with bow and arrow, indeed when they were fought merely with TNT, national withdrawal, national isolation, national indifference were all possible. But a nuclear war would probably be not just the last war; it would indisputably be the first real *world* war.

Thus:

> The Canadians have experienced the political tensions of the cold war and been faced with the requirements of collective defense at the very moment when they would have preferred to devote their total energies to building an industrial nation and exploiting vast natural resources. Their great undertakings were giving fresh meaning to the term "Canadianism" just when the demands of the cold war required that they submerge their particular interests to some extent in the greater interests of the free world.[1]

Canada, and Canada alone, is a nation sandwiched between giant nuclear powers. Whatever its search for a policy in world affairs, its role in the geography of world affairs is fixed. Whatever the claims made upon it in the name of national independence, the claims made upon it in the name of continental interdependence for defense cannot be denied.

But U.S.–Canadian defense relations are not merely the product of geography tempered by nuclear realities. History has shaped them too. An accurate description of Canadian defense policy today might be that Canada has its "obligations as a good friendly neighbour, and one of them is to see . . . should the occasion ever arise, enemy forces should not be able to pursue their way, either by land, sea or air to the United States across Canadian territory." Obviously relevant today, that was the statement of Prime Minister MacKenzie King in 1938.[2]

In 1938, President Roosevelt declared that the United States "will not stand idly by if domination of Canadian soil is threatened by any other empire." [3] And the same theme is repeated today—as in the Canadian White Paper on Defence of March 1964:

It is, for the foreseeable future, impossible to conceive of any significant external threat to Canada which is not also a threat to North America as a whole. It is equally inconceivable that, in resisting clear and unequivocal aggression against Canadian territory, Canada could not rely on the active support of the United States.[4]

The threat is more real, the weapons more awful, Canadian resentment undoubtedly more avid. But the basic continental interdependence for defense stems from a common history of reaction to aggression, a common recognition of the necessity of deterrence, a common set of values which make us allies with or without an alliance and interdependent with or without friendship.

Why was 1938 the turning point? The international and military policies of the two countries have evolved in a similar fashion. Nineteenth-century United States was preoccupied with the development of its western lands and only with the turn of the century did its nationalism turn outward in search of its own international role. The Canadian preoccupation with the development of its Dominion and essential indiffer-

61

ence to world affairs lasted until the eve of World War II.

For each, World War I taught separate lessons, which when combined formed the basis for a continental defense arrangement. To the United States, World War I taught the lesson, which we were slow to learn, that in an age of weapons of mass destruction, international dependence was a necessity. The United States, by choosing to stay outside of the League of Nations which it had been so instrumental in creating, ignored the lesson that was so clear—even though it had been written indelibly on the conscience of every American.

Perhaps the dominant lesson of World War I to Canadians was that "a common defence policy for the Commonwealth just would not work." [5] So while the Americans were learning of the necessity of interdependence, the Canadians were learning that interdependence based upon history, but not geography, a common heritage but not a common foe, gave little assurance.

Just as the American isolation from the League of Nations showed that they had not learned the lessons the "Great War" had taught, so too did Canada seem intent on allowing an illusion to prevent a continental defense arrangement, which only the immediacy of World War II would make a reality. This illusion, of all things, was the possibility of an attack by the armed forces of the United States on Canada itself. For ten years, from 1921 to 1931, the operations of the Canadian armed forces were guided by "Defence Scheme No. 1" which envisaged an American invasion. This incredible document described the likely U.S. strategy.

> The main objective of the United States force would undoubtedly be Montreal and on to Ottawa. The next important objective of the United States would be the occupation of the Ontario Peninsula, including the cities of Hamilton and Toronto. The other objectives at which the American Land Forces would be moved against would be Quebec, Winnipeg, the Island of Vancouver and South Western British Columbia, i.e., the area including Vancouver and New Westminster.

The grain-growing Provinces of Manitoba, Saskatchewan, and Alberta which now have a large percentage of Americans, are especially attractive to the United States, and there is just a possibility that they might make the conquest of these Provinces the ultimate objective of their campaign . . .[6]

The "Defence Scheme No. 1" then pinpointed Canadian counterobjectives: The Pacific Command was to "occupy the strategic points including Spokane, Seattle, and Portland, Oregon"; the Prairie Command was to "converge towards Fargo" and then "continue a general advance in the direction of Minneapolis and St. Paul"; the Great Lakes Command was to make "raids . . . across the Niagara Frontier, the St. Clair Frontier, the Detroit Frontier and the St. Mary's Frontier, with sufficient troops to establish bridgeheads"; the Quebec Command was to "take the offensive on both sides of the Adirondack Mountains with a view of converging . . . in the vicinity of Albany, N.Y."; and the Maritime Command was "to make an offensive into the State of Maine."

Surely the number of Canadians who shared the fantastic nightmare of the author of "Defence Scheme No. 1" was even smaller than the number of Americans who seriously espoused annexation. But until the torch was put to the copies of this secret document in 1931, it was official Canadian policy. Small wonder that no joint continental defense plans were forged in the interwar period.

But the lessons of World War I were more compelling than the imagination of a few extremists, and it bordered on the inevitable that with the advent of the second total war, the two countries would form bonds of continental defense that have secured their lands ever since. With the declarations of 1938, with the creation of the Joint Board of Defense in Ogdensburg, New York, in 1940, with the common planning for the defense of the North American continent the two countries established a pattern of cooperation which could not be ended by the end of the war.

It is important for Americans to appreciate that the pattern of cooperation for defense established in World War II included, even then, a Canadian resentment—stemming from just cause. The military strategy of the Allies was formulated by the Anglo-American Combined Chiefs of Staff. Despite the Canadian contribution of more than 1 million men in uniform—and 42,000 dead—the Canadians were not included in the meetings of the Combined Chiefs of Staff, and apparently the United States continued to believe that when Britain spoke it spoke for Canada as well. U.S.–Canadian cooperation, even with the best of motives on both sides of the border, was attended by the aggravating and familiar American inclination to take Canada for granted.

And it is not unimportant to realize that Canada was the only Allied nation to which the United States extended no direct aid. Quite the contrary, Canada shared with the U.S. the financial burden of the Allied venture as no other country did, by providing $3.5 billion of aid to the Allies. Not only did Canada not need financial assistance from the United States, but in fact it was the U.S. that was dependent upon Canadian natural resources to produce the one great weapon which finally ended World War II and plunged the world into a nuclear age.

The legacy thus left by World War II was a blend of diverse trends. First, and foremost, was the experience of continental cooperation—and the continuing institutions of cooperation. Second was the recognized need of interdependence produced not just by the emergence of the nuclear age but by the unavoidable fact that World War II had no better chance to be the "war to end all wars" than had World War I. Third was the growth of Canadian nationalism with its resentment of American domination and what seemed to them the annoying American habits. And fourth was the growth, with the blessing and work of both nations, of a truly effective attempt at international cooperation through the United Nations.

In 1947, rather than repeating the appalling isolation that followed World War I, the United States, Britain, and Canada proved that this time they not only had been taught but had learned some lessons. The Anglo-American Joint Chiefs of Staff were joined by the Canadian Government in declaring that while each country would maintain sovereignty over its territory, it would continue to maintain full military cooperation. And the Joint Board of Defense was made the Permanent Joint Board of Defense.

Thus in 1948, when the Soviet Union and the international Communist movement had proven themselves to be bent upon the domination of all of Europe that they could get, the cooperation of the ABC powers provided a natural foundation for the development of the North Atlantic Treaty Organization. Once again a common foe had arisen in Europe, and once again Britain, isolated by a channel, and Canada and the United States, isolated by an ocean, joined with the nations of Europe for their common defense. Never again would they be so foolish as to ignore the small fires of Europe in the belief that they would not be engulfed by the flames. And when the sudden Communist aggression struck in Korea, they proved again that they had learned the lessons that in the 1930's had been taught with such devastating finality to mankind.

The greatest test of the strength of the U.S.–Canadian defense partnership emerged with the growth of the Soviet nuclear capacity. As long as only the United States had nuclear weapons, the world and Canada and the United States seemed safe from annihilation. But Soviet nuclear power was different. Western man knew that if he could not deter a Soviet nuclear attack on the United States, he could not assure the future. Every Canadian knew that defense against a nuclear attack on the United States would result in the world's most climactic battle in the air over Canadian soil. And every thoughtful Canadian knew too that to avoid that battle, to deter attack, would require the closest cooperation between the North American democracies.

With their reluctance to tie themselves so closely to the United States matched only by their wisdom in accepting the necessary, the Canadians in the 1950's entered upon an extra-ordinary adventure in enlightened generosity. They allowed their country to become another's first line of defense through a network of radar, ballistic-missile early-warning systems, and a variety of air-surveillance plans. A nuclear-age trip-wire was strung across Canada from Alaska to Greenland. In 1957, this effort in cooperative nuclear deterrence became institutional-ized in the North American Air Defense Command—NORAD —at once the symbol of devastating destruction for any enemy and the object of Canadian anti-U.S. sentiment. It is typical of U.S.–Canadian relations to realize that while NORAD to most Canadians is the most blatant example of the interdependence they cannot avoid, it is almost totally unknown in the United States. In a poll of 1,000 high-school seniors in the American states bordering on Canada, only 70, or 7 per cent, could identify NORAD.

NORAD consists of 170,000 personnel in 400 bases. Ninety-four per cent of these men are Americans. Canada contributes approximately $115 million to its budget—and the United States $2 billion, or seventeen times as much.

Many Americans may ask the question: "Why do the Cana-dians complain about NORAD? We are supplying most of the money. We are supplying most of the men." It is important to understand that $115 million is 8 per cent of the total Canadian defense budget, while $2 billion is barely 4 per cent of the total U.S. defense budget. But it is even more important to understand that in a very real sense the Canadian contribution cannot be measured in money or in men, for the Canadian contribution is their future as a nation.

Through NORAD, Canada sacrifices the capacity to pursue a fully independent course. Through NORAD, Canada sacri-fices the ability to influence fully other nations by an indepen-dence from the United States. Through NORAD, Canada commits itself as the one sure battleground in a nuclear-age exchange between the powers that face each other across her land. To Canadians it is of small consolation that geography and technology give them no alternative.

James Minifie asks: "Shall Canada's role be that of powder-monkey or peacemaker?" He would have Canada dissolve NORAD, withdraw from NATO, annul the Permanent Joint Board of Defense, and seek a Canadian destiny within the Commonwealth of Nations and the United Nations. To Minifie, "the vivid and memorable act which would set the stage for the restoration of Canadian independence would be a Declaration of Neutrality." [7] And he goes further:

> The Polar threat has been exaggerated. Canada could meet it alone, by inflicting unacceptable losses on bombers without the bondage of NORAD. The policy of deterrence through massive retaliation has been a gigantic hoax. [8]

Let the Canadians be the first to answer Canadians. Professor Alastair Taylor of Queen's University:

> Whether or not Canadians believe themselves to be involved with John Donne in all mankind, it should be obvious that if any piece of the North American continent be attacked or captured, our own status and security will to that extent be diminished. In other words, we cannot contract out of geography, which has made Canada a buffer zone between two super-powers. Consequently, the United States is not less involved than this country in continental defence. [9]

Posit for a moment a world in which ideological adversaries, each with nuclear weapons, were also neighbors. That day may come in the future, and it may impose a test upon man which may make today's world seem only like a routine fire drill.

Of all the blessings of history, men should be most thankful for one which has been little noted: The nations that have chosen to develop national nuclear weapons have, when separated by ideology, also been separated by distance. Distance may seem little in the face of the modern capacity to deliver annihilation. And it may seem little in terms of time—but that time, even twenty minutes' time, is the most precious commodity on earth today. For twenty minutes' time can assure that a victim will know he is being attacked, that he can prepare to defend himself no matter how incompletely, and, most important, that he can retaliate.

It is that time, that precious twenty minutes of time, which allows the American deterrent force to deter. The DEW line, the BMEWS, NORAD—these are the means of providing that time. And they are the symbol to the Soviet Union that whatever its intention, it cannot attack the North American continent without reaping unto itself a veritable Armageddon.

Deterrence is made real only by the availability of time to retaliate. This is the meaning of NORAD and BMEWS. Without them the advantage of time is lost, and the confidence in deterrence is lost. Canada has no more choice than the United States, for with or without BMEWS, with or without NORAD, if there is a battle to stop a Soviet nuclear attack on the United States, it will be fought over Canadian territory. If the attack is by plane, it will be intercepted over Canada. If the attack is by missile, it will be intercepted over Canada. This is the harsh, unavoidable, unchangeable, and irrefutable fact of North American defense. And so Canadians and Canada must pray even more fervently than most for deterrence, and must contribute to it. U.S. nuclear power plus time—twenty minutes' time—is today the only deterrence we know. And only Canada can provide that time.

So much for the harsh fact facing Canada. What is the harsh fact facing the United States? It is the reality of anti-Americanism that NORAD creates. No doubt it stems in part from the frustration of an absence of Canadian choice—that in this one sphere the United States can in fact take Canada for granted because she has no rational choice. But nations before have acted irrationally and against their own best interest. And it is not inconceivable that if the United States continues to ignore Canadian fears, anti-Americanism will grow in Canada to the point where emotions dominate reason, and NORAD is suddenly dissolved. The terms of the agreement allow its dissolution at any time by either party.

James Minifie has described the formula by which Canadian resentment grows: ". . . nobody chalks 'Yankee Go Home' on the walls. Nobody waves the bloody shirt. So the American concludes, happily but wrongly, that there is no anti-Americanism in Canada." [10] In our refusal to notice the Canadian resentment we merely contribute further to it.

NORAD has been allowed to dominate in the thinking about Canadian–U.S. defense policy. It amounts to a very small part of the defense budgets of each nation. Coordinated operations within NORAD should not be confused with integration of the military forces of the two countries. The Honorable Arnold Heeney, in addressing the Fifth Windsor Seminar on U.S.–Canadian relations, concluded:

> The Royal Canadian Air Force and the United States Air Force are not unified. They are certainly integrated for the purposes of NORAD as NORAD serves two governments and not one. If NORAD serves two governments and not one, the elements which compose that command, although integrated for certain purposes, are certainly not unified. If they were unified we would not discuss Canadian-American relations, we would be discussing United States policy only. [11]

It is to the interest of both governments to emphasize the operations of other joint defense consultative arrangements—such as the Permanent Joint Board of Defense and the Cabinet Committee on Joint Defense. These two institutions are advisory, whereas NORAD has administrative power. These two consultative organs should be the primary channels of defense communications between the two countries. We do not wish to minimize the significance of NORAD, nor do we wish to belittle the obligation of its commanders to assure full recognition of the Canadian voice. But we believe it imperative to preserve the psychological framework within which NORAD can con-

69

tinue to be tolerated by the Canadian people. It is increasingly important for the United States to consult with Canada on basic defense decisions rather than to adopt a course which Canada is then forced to follow. This means consultation through the Cabinet Committee and the Joint Board.

There is, of course, one conceivable alternative for Canada to NORAD and North American Defense coordination. That would be the development of an independent Canadian nuclear force, which could provide its own deterrent to nuclear attack. In 1963, an extensive public-opinion poll in Canada showed that fully 75 per cent of the population believed that over half of all Canadians would be killed in a nuclear war with Russia.[12] Nonetheless only 17 per cent of all Canadians expressed the feeling that under no circumstances should Canada develop the bomb itself. Three out of every four Canadian businessmen favored the development of a Canadian nuclear force.[13]

The single greatest problem facing mankind today is the proliferation of the knowledge needed to build nuclear weapons. History shows undeniably that the production costs of every item inevitably diminish, and that production techniques inevitably simplify. It will in time be possible for a relatively rich man, and any country, to produce The Bomb. At the rate of growth of our technology, it will not be long before a do-it-yourself nuclear-bomb kit will enable the flowering of a plethora of backyard Caesars. Those with an appreciation of the geometric growth of technology, those who have learned from history, and those who have vision know that this decade is the world's last chance to avoid the descent to an incredible nuclear holocaust—or a paranoid world so wracked by fear that reason will die.

To this date, the five nations who have chosen to develop nuclear weapons have all been great powers through history—long before they have been nuclear powers. No middle power, no developing power, has yet sought and achieved nuclear-weapons capacity. With each addition to the nuclear club, the

70

restraints on those who have denied themselves that distinction grow less. And if a middle power or a developing country acquires its own nuclear weapons, the prestige race will be on. That is why it is the responsibility of the United States, the other nuclear powers, and all other responsible nations to give an unmistakable priority above all other policy to the necessity for an end to nuclear proliferation.

In the inevitable crisis atmosphere in which the State Department in Washington must operate, long-term policy considerations seldom achieve the attention they deserve. Nowhere has this been more evident than in the field of arms control and disarmament. Some international crises fester over years until circumstances or men or memories change to allow an amicable resolution. But the spread of nuclear weapons is a problem which, if allowed to fester, will only become more severe. Time without action is not its healer—it is the undoing of us all.

There is, of course, an unavoidable discrimination in any reasonable solution to the nuclear-proliferation problem. Short of general and complete disarmament, which is as far from reality today as it ever has been, any solution to nuclear proliferation will leave some nations with and some without the greatest power ever known to man. It is almost psychologically impossible for the "haves" to preach effectively to the "have-nots." Arms control is one area where the Canadian capacity for initiative and influence in foreign affairs becomes an obligation.

The Toronto *Globe and Mail,* noting Canadian supply of uranium to the United States and its own desires for great-power status, likened Canada unto "the dope peddler who is on the verge of becoming an addict. It is of some significance that the dope peddler is generally deplored more than the addict." [14] However much uranium she supplied, Canada did not drop the bombs on Hiroshima and Nagasaki. However much capacity she may have to build a nuclear weapon, Canada has not done so. And because she, perhaps above all

71

nonnuclear nations, has the industrial base, the technical know-how, and the raw materials, Canadian abstinence can be a powerful influence on those other nations who may be tempted to seek great-power status through instant great power.

If either or both of our nations were to extend to the problems of nuclear proliferation the priority they deserve, the policy initiatives available could be dramatic:

(a.) The unilateral offer—if necessary, unmatched by equivalent Soviet wisdom—to place all peaceful nuclear facilities on the North American continent under the international inspection and safeguard system of the International Atomic Energy Agency. This is in effect what the United States asks all nonnuclear powers to accept through a nonproliferation agreement. But the United States bargaining position is a weak one if we are unwilling to submit ourselves to the kind of inspection which we ask others to accept. It is not possible for the United States to submit its military nuclear facilities to inspection on a unilateral basis, but it need have no fear to submit its peaceful nuclear facilities to international inspection under the proven system of the IAEA.

(b.) The establishment, perhaps again through the International Atomic Energy Agency, of a consortium to sell fissionable material for peaceful purposes at artificially reduced prices. Any IAEA sales would be made conditional upon acceptance of IAEA safeguard inspection systems. The United States and Canada alone could provide sufficient uranium for the international market through IAEA to assure an ample supply for generations to come without depleting their own resources to the point of potential impairment of national security. Some potential nuclear powers have available resources of fissionable material. For example, India boasts a plentiful supply of thorium. The mining and production costs are very great, however. If fissionable material in plentiful supply were available at significantly lower cost through an international consortium, there would be meaningful domestic pressures in India and all other potential nuclear powers to purchase the material through the IAEA even at the expense of accepting the safeguards and

72

inspection system that would accompany it. This proposal would encourage the peaceful development of nuclear power and the acceptance of international standards of inspection.

(c.) Canada and the United States, as major donors of foreign aid, are in a unique position to initiate negotiations leading to a binding agreement by all foreign-aid contributor nations to cut off all foreign assistance to any nation that develops nuclear weapons. Up to this point, except for the fleeting disfavor of world public opinion, there is no sanction applied to a nation that chooses to develop an independent nuclear capacity. But the spread of nuclear weapons is too dangerous for the world to avoid harsh penalties for those who would bring Armageddon closer. Such a cut-off of foreign aid can be justified not only in the search for a safe world, but because a developing nation has no business utilizing its precious resources in the development of nuclear weapons rather than in programs of economic progress. This kind of sanctions program would be practical only if all the nuclear powers and foreign-aid-giving powers were to participate. Only a simultaneous aid cut-off from the United States, the Soviet Union, and all other aid-giving nations would be a sufficient threat to convince a potential nuclear power of the severity of the decision before it.

These initiatives would be bold steps—but the dangers that the world confronts require boldness. None of them alone nor all of them together represents sufficient progress. They must be matched, of course, by consistent and undaunted efforts to achieve a universal nonproliferation agreement, the negotiation of atom-free zones, the extension of some form of security to those nations who may feel that they need nuclear weapons to assure their security, and meaningful evidence that the United States and the Soviet Union (if not Communist China also) are willing to engage in a program not merely to cut off further development of their own nuclear-weapon stockpiles but to cut back the stockpiles they already have.

The initiatives of Canada and the United States acting in concert—or of Canada acting alone—can be immense in a world which craves a commitment to a safe and sane future. Our only choice is clear; our only chance is now. The history of the "second hundred years" may be written on this one issue alone.

The last great entry on the agenda of Canadian–American defense questions is the future of NATO. From a Canadian perspective, it is inseparable from the search for national identity. It is part and parcel of the question whether Canada can and should be an active member of the Western Hemisphere, or the North Atlantic Community, or the British Commonwealth of Nations, or the United Nations, or all or any combination thereof.

The Honorable Paul Martin, Secretary of State for External Affairs, in an address in Cleveland, Ohio, in March 1965, stated the three basic elements of Canadian defense policy in forthright and simple terms:

> *First,* a contribution of ground, air and naval forces to Western Europe and the North Atlantic;
> *Second,* a contribution to North American air defence through NORAD;
> *Third,* a contribution to international peace keeping through the United Nations.[15]

But despite the high priority of the Canadian commitment to the North Atlantic community, Canada today is searching the same horizon that American policy-makers scan in the desperate struggle for the means to keep the North Atlantic Alliance together. The United States and Canada returned to the European continent in the late 1940's in order to provide the capacity to defend Europe until such time as she could economically and militarily defend herself. In great measure, the annoyances of General de Gaulle and the independence of the European allies, which we in the United States tend to bemoan so much, are proof of the success of earlier North American policies. But now that Europe does stand on its own feet, we, or at least we in the United States, find that we don't like it too much.

74

What is the ultimate resolution of the NATO conflict? And does it (should it) include a continuing role for the United States and Canada, their troops, and their commitment?

The North American commitment to the defense of Europe —and principally the commitment of United States nuclear power if necessary—is of course the shield behind which General de Gaulle can afford to demonstrate his independence. Without the assurance of North American power for defense, Western Europe could not explore, as it is now beginning to explore, a resolution of the Central European division, and the creation of what De Gaulle calls "a Europe to the Urals." NATO's continued existence is a necessity—even to and for De Gaulle. Just as NATO achieved a reduction of the Soviet military threat in Europe, its continued existence will assure that the threat will not arise again.

Now, as the political destiny of Europe evolves, NATO can be made into a more positive force—the means through which the North Atlantic community can negotiate on the European continent for the creation of a Europe united through trade and political association. In this development, as well as in the military alliance, the commitment of the United States and Canada is an invaluable source of strength, for it means that no one in Europe need ever doubt that the power alliance that was victorious in two world wars remains intact to avoid a third. And it means that we shall not allow ourselves to recede gradually to the illusion of safe isolation we once thought we had found.

Canada, in an undeniable sense, plays a vital role in the determination of U.S. choices and in the maintenance of North Atlantic ties. If Canada were to withdraw from Europe, would we remain alone? And perhaps just as crucial for the future of NATO, if Canada were to withdraw, would not the Europeans believe that the United States would be quick to follow? Again it is a commitment and an interest which by history, by origin, and by the perils of a nuclear world we share in common.

We must share in common also the knowledge that the solution of NATO's problems and the future of a united Europe can come only from the free consultation of free and independent nations. We cannot dictate from North America the course of Europe even if we wished to. We in the United States cannot dictate the NATO course of Canada. For an alliance, particularly an alliance with the outside threat seeming to diminish with each passing year, cannot survive a leader who leads by fiat. Patient and quiet diplomacy, through the multitude of joint consultative processes, is the recipe for sane progress within the North Atlantic Community.

MacKenzie King said of the Ogdensburg Agreement in 1941 that it was "no temporary Axis, formed by nations whose common tie was a mutual desire for the destruction of their neighbors. The Hyde Park Declaration is, I believe, a further convincing demonstration that Canada and the United States are indeed laying the enduring foundations of a new world order, an order based on international understanding, on mutual aid, on friendship and good will." [16]

International understanding, mutual aid, friendship and good will, in the realm of defense, require of Canada some acceptance of the needs and realities of deterrence in the nuclear age. Of the United States they require a greater recognition of Canada's role in our own security. When we take Canada for granted, we take our security for granted—and neither is a wise or promising course.

It is dubious consolation to the Canadian people to know that in a nuclear attack, we will always be at their side. But we hope that it will be more than geography that puts us there. We hope to be at their side in the cause of peace, not just in the scourge of war. We hope to be at their side in serving the needs of men. We hope to be at their side in building on the North American continent a durable model for relations between and among independent nations—attentive to the national interests of each, devoted to the prosperity of both, compassionate toward the human needs of all.

Chapter V

Canada in Her Hemisphere

When George Canning "called in the New World to redress the balance of the Old," he underlined for today's historian one of the three dominant facts in the development of the modern Western Hemisphere. Every single country in this New World has been shaped in part by the national imperialism and the individual adventurism of Europe.

The second dominant fact of the history of the Western Hemisphere is that most of its countries have been severed from Europe by force. The third is that those so separated have banded together in an Inter-American system.

Of the 500 million people in the Western Hemisphere, who are those that are not in the political structure of their hemisphere? Cuba's Old World ties were slashed by a jingoistic display of American nationalism before the turn of the century, but have now been replaced by the undeniable foreign influence of international Communism. French Guiana and the French islands in the Caribbean remain Departments of France. Guyana has only recently achieved "peaceful," if tumultuous, independence from the British Crown. British Honduras will follow in due time, as Jamaica and Trinidad and Tobago had preceded. And finally Canada, whose independence from the Old World was similarly evolutionary, has remained outside the hemispheric organization.

It is not by accident that this line-up of nations outside the Inter-American system leads inescapably to memories of the Monroe Doctrine. It is important for those who would be quick to criticize the extent of Canadian involvement in the affairs of her hemisphere to realize that until well after the Statute of Westminster in 1931, which guaranteed Canada the right to an independent foreign and defense policy, the nations of the Inter-American system considered Canadian ties to Great Britain and the Commonwealth of Nations as insurmountable obstacles to her membership in the New World organization.

Yesterday the hemisphere's nations imposed upon Canada the same choice that she faces today. Either her destiny will be found as an independent member of the Inter-American system, or she will pursue her national identity with the British Commonwealth of Nations. She cannot be part of the Old World and the New World too. Where does her course lie?

The Organization of American States, the central body of the Inter-American system, technically was founded in 1948, but it is merely the successor to the Pan-American Union, founded in 1910, which, in its turn, was merely the successor to the Commercial Bureau of the Americas, established in 1899. Through most of that history, Canada, with its independence coming only in peaceful stages from the British, and with its quick entry into two world wars at the British side as evidence, was considered too closely tied to the Old World to be acceptable in the institutions of the new. Indeed it was not until after World War II, in 1947 and 1948, that there was Inter-American discussion about changing the term "republic" to "state" in the Charter of the Pan-American Union to facilitate Canadian membership. But:

> National independence through a document such as the Statute of Westminster would have been as historically impossible for the emerging republics of Latin America as it was for the United States. Canada's national role of political compromise as a North American monarchy, which has absorbed many of the constitutional techniques of both the modern British monarchy and the modern American federal structures thus appears to have impeded easy and close association with the OAS.[1]

Both before and after the emergence of the Hoover-Roosevelt thesis of good neighborhood in the Western Hemisphere, the United States itself opposed Canadian entry into the Inter-American system. In its instructions to the U.S. delegation at the 1927 Conference for Canadian Admission at Havana, the United States Secretary of State included the following:

> If colonies . . . or dominions whose foreign relations are controlled by European states were represented . . . the influence . . . of European powers would be injected into the . . . disposition of questions affecting the political entities of this hemisphere. Should Canada be proposed as a member, you will be guided by the oral instructions given by the Secretary of State to the delegation . . .[2]

The oral instructions were opposed to Canadian membership.

The moving force for a good-neighbor policy within the Roosevelt Administration was Sumner Welles, who said in 1936 that "there is no more logical reason why Canada should be represented in the Pan American Union than Jamaica, or . . . British, French or Dutch Guiana."[3] It is easy to forget, now, when Canadian membership in the OAS seems desirable and natural to almost all Americans, that the twenty years since the end of World War II were preceded by fifty years of United States policy that not only opposed Canadian membership, but directed U.S. diplomats in Latin America to do what they could to avoid Latin initiatives in this direction.

Unfortunately, one short-sighted United States policy was replaced with another. Opposition to Canadian membership was replaced by a virtual demand for Canadian membership. A policy that assumed that Canadian foreign policy was written in London was replaced with a policy that assumed that Canadian foreign policy could be written in Washington. There can be little doubt that despite the highest motivation behind his effort, President Kennedy's lecture to the Canadian Parliament in May 1961 on their responsibilities to engage in the Inter-American system hurt his cause.

All this history, together with U.S. journalism's inattention to the details of Canadian foreign relations, has combined to leave the impression in the minds of the U.S. public that it is Canadian policy not to have anything whatsoever to do with affairs in Latin America. It may be constructive therefore to review the extensive relations which Canada has in fact established throughout the hemisphere. Canada has representatives in every Latin American country where there are U.S. representatives. Of the more than sixty Canadian diplomatic missions around the world, a quarter of them are in her own hemisphere.

While not a member of the Organization of American States, she is a member of the Pan-American Institute of Geography and History, the Inter-American Statistical Institute, and the Pan American Radio Office. She sends observers as representatives to all significant meetings of the Organization of American States, to many special meetings of the Alliance for Progress, to meetings of the U.N. Economic Commission for Latin America, and to a variety of other specialized meetings on subjects of common importance.

She has constantly been increasing her trade missions, composed of business and government officials visiting in Latin America. She has important new Latin American study centers at several Canadian universities.

Perhaps most importantly, she is participating actively in aid and development programs in the hemisphere. She has extended significant development grants to the British Commonwealth areas in the Caribbean—the West Indies, British Honduras, Guyana, Jamaica, and Trinidad and Tobago. She has made significant disbursement loans to Mexico, Argentina, and other Latin American countries. While not a member of the Inter-American Development Bank, her participation in that institution has been significantly increased in recent years.

But all this participation in the hemisphere has fallen far short of a deliberate decision by the Canadian people and Canadian Government to dive headlong into the new world of turmoil which Latin America and her relations with the United States represent. The present Canadian Foreign Minister, when his party was the opposition party, believed that Canadian in-

80

terests should be pursued through membership in the OAS. With the responsibilities of power, both Mr. Martin and his party have become more cautious. Both he and, later, Prime Minister Pearson, have at Banff suggested that their inclination is to lead Canada into the Organization of American States. But the government has fallen short of a full commitment for membership.

To most Americans the reasons for the Canadian hesitation seem obscure. They may not fully appreciate the immensity of the decision which rests before the Canadian people and its government. In a very real sense, the decision to join or not to join the Organization of American States represents for Canada a fundamental definition of the national identity that it intends to pursue. The arguments lined up against OAS membership and full-scale participation in the Inter-American system are manifold.

The first set of arguments relates to the alternative courses for the definition of Canadian identity and purpose in international relations. Should the future of Canada be tied to the Inter-American system or to the British Commonwealth of Nations—or to the United Nations or some other international grouping—or to some combination of groupings?

In large measure, the structure of Canada's non–U.S. trade, the make-up of her foreign-aid program, and the instinct of her political ties have been directed more toward the Commonwealth nations than toward the hemisphere. As British colonial rule has evolved into a world-wide system of independent nations, and as those independent nations have seemed to draw farther and farther apart across economic and political gulfs, the Canadian Government and the Canadian people have faced a difficult decision in charting a new international course. Full-fledged Canadian membership and participation in the institutions and program of the Inter-American system would inevitably require subordinate Canadian decisions to establish new trade patterns, new aid patterns, and new lines of political interest.

To many it appears that the sun which once never set on the

British Empire is now making its last slow descent on the Commonwealth as an effective force in international politics. Its political integrity has long since evaporated. The economic and trade ties are increasingly difficult to maintain in their once dominant form. Only the history books, language, and a Queen hold these nations together. The similarity of the national interests of Britain and India, of Canada and Ghana, of Nigeria and Australia, of South Africa and Guyana, are small and getting smaller. The age of imperial rule, no matter how enlightened that rule may have been, has inevitably given way to an even more enlightened age of free and independent peoples.

In an era of pluralism and incredible danger, any positive ties that hold different national peoples together and at peace are a source of stability in an unstable world. But it does no injustice to the history of the British Commonwealth to suggest that in the future it may be a less promising source of international progress than it has been in the past.

Perhaps in 1936 Sumner Welles could conclude that Canadian membership in the hemispheric institutions was no more logical than that of Jamaica or British Guiana. It now seems inevitable that these countries will join the Inter-American system—and then the question of logic might seem to be quite reversed.

As long as there is a Britain, there will be a British Commonwealth. But surely Commonwealth membership is not incompatible with participation in other international groupings whose purpose is no less progressive than that of the British and British foreign policy itself.

Each of the Commonwealth members, including Canada, faces a decision not unlike that which confronts each young man and woman in this world of extraordinarily rapid change. The values, the ideals, and memories to which the parent clings provide a momentous dilemma for the offspring anxious to set out on his own in a world different from that of his parents. The values, traditions, and memories of the parents are seldom wrong, only increasingly irrelevant in the world of their children. In families of people, and in families of nations, the best solution is generally found when the parent has the wisdom to let the child go his own way and the child has the wisdom to establish an independent identity without irrevocably severing his ties from the sources of his own personality.

What of the United Nations? Will the Canadians decide that their devotion to the internationalism of the U.N. would be compromised by their participation in the regionalism of the hemisphere? It is understandable that the Canadians are reluctant to engage fully in the operation of a collective regional-defense system which may at times appear to be in conflict with the interest and global preoccupation of the United Nations. Certainly the most visible contribution of the independent postwar Canadian foreign policy has been the promotion of the ideals and institutions of the U.N. And there can be no doubt that upon occasion the interests of the nations of the Western Hemisphere will not be identical with those of the Eastern Hemisphere.

But the United Nations long since would have faltered and folded if it had not embraced at its outset sufficient flexibility to permit variances in national and regional interests. It is too much to ask of a world built upon the nation-state principle to pass suddenly to a genuine and universal internationalism. Whatever our dreams for the evolution of the United Nations— whatever our hopes for an ultimate world where national boundaries will seem unnecessary—that world today is no more than a dream to pursue over generations to come, not a tangible possibility within our reach.

In rational pursuit of the dream of internationalism, regional coordination and cooperation is a practical and progressive step toward creation of a flexible international body with a supranational authority which may one day evolve. Thus while the very slow and painful evolution of Europe toward greater unity may on occasion appear to be in conflict with the universalism of the United Nations, it is a meaningful and real step toward the institutions of peace. And the Inter-American sys-

83

tem, whatever its shortcomings—and it has many—and whatever its potential conflicts and disagreements with the United Nations, is a step in the same direction—a painful and sometimes uncertain step, but a progressive step nonetheless.

The late Dag Hammarskjöld used to remind the newly independent and developing members that the U.N. was more necessary for them than it was for the great powers. The Latin Americans surely see the United Nations as an institution to safeguard their interest; but they know as well that hemispheric regionalism can be an even more sure safeguard of their security and even more valuable catalyst for their progress. Progress in regionalism and universalism in the OAS and the U.N. are inseparable from each other. What damages either hurts the other. What serves the interests of one gives impetus to them both.

Some Canadians have argued that since fully one third of the Canadian population is of French descent, a potential course of Canadian foreign policy would be involvement with the former French colonial areas, just as the British descendants would argue for association with the former British colonial areas. Surely the argument, however, is less impressive than the suggestion that the Latin cultural heritage of one third of all Canadians leads directly to a tie within its hemisphere to peoples who share that heritage.

The second category of argument against Canadian membership in the inter-American organizations is that it is undesirable for Canada to involve itself in the political problems of the hemisphere even though it may wish to engage in the economic growth and progress of Latin America. The argument goes that Canadian national identity might best be pursued by a vigorous delve into the development of the hemisphere—but a judicious restraint from participation in its politics. And some would add to the theory the corollary that Canadian influence as a mediator in international disputes relies on her independence of binding political associations: ". . . experience has shown in the Congo, Indo-China and elsewhere, that countries outside of a region of serious problems have frequently been able to play a more constructive role in helping to resolve the problems than those which are closer and more closely involved—thus, as regards Latin American problems, Canada can potentially play a more constructive role as an independent nation in the hemisphere." [4]

Others have suggested that this argument is a mere rationalization for avoiding the harsh realities of the world in which Canada finds itself. They point out that the economics of the hemisphere and the politics of the hemisphere are inseparable —and that both are fundamentally shaped by the decisions of the institutions of the Inter-American system. They conclude that the only way for Canada to contribute economically to the development of Latin America without participating in the political discourse within the hemisphere is to give unparalleled funds without sufficient concern for their use to join the inevitable political debate over the best course to progress. And their final counterargument is that however valuable a mediating role Canada can play between conflicting nations of the world, that role is minimized in the hemisphere by the common resentment of any conflicting parties to the fact that she is a member of their hemisphere only in a geographic sense. Canada, they argue, cannot be part of two worlds; it cannot mediate as an outsider when it lives inside; it cannot mask its location in the New World by pretending to bring the impartial diplomacy of the Old.

Nonetheless there is a distinct trend among Latin American governments to wish to separate more effectively the economic and political institutions of the hemisphere. And if Canada should choose to follow a path of gradually increased participation in the affairs of her hemisphere, it may be possible for her in time to join the economic institutions without joining the political institutions. It would remain to be seen whether membership in the one sphere would not lead inevitably to pressures to participate in the other.

But of all the arguments against Canadian membership in the Inter-American system, none is more potent in Canada nor more important for Americans to appreciate than the following:

85

The OAS is thoroughly infiltrated, controlled and oriented by the United States, whose creation it is. The American voice is his master's voice. Some Latin American countries have largely freed themselves from Washington, but none has ever made the OAS anything but the U.S.'s instrument.

By becoming a member, Canada accepts one more prodding-stick. As in NATO and NORAD, unanimity rules and the unanimity is American.

Our country has no need to belong to the OAS to improve her relations with Latin America. As for her relations with the United States, they are so good that if they were to become ever-so-slightly better we would have to hoist the Stars and Stripes on the Peace Tower . . .[5]

A brief review of the highlights of American policy in Latin America over the past six years might be instructive in appreciating the source of Canadian concern.

The Bay of Pigs invasion of Cuba in 1961, which preceded President Kennedy's OAS membership speech to the Canadian Parliament by only one month, was of course a military fiasco. In the minds of some, it may well have been a moral fiasco. But the point to be made here is that to many in the OAS and to many in Canada it was a political fiasco, in that it was conceived and executed without the approval or even the knowledge of the Organization of American States. The institution created at the urging of the United States for the express purpose of collective security within the Hemisphere, was totally ignored in a unilateral military action. The Canadians ask: "Isn't it true that the OAS is merely an organization which the United States uses for its purposes to force the Latins into line when it can, and ignores when it assumes that the Latins cannot be forced into line?"

In December 1961, the OAS voted by majority rule at the Punta del Este Conference to expel Cuba from membership. It is no secret that the U.S. Goverment applied extraordinary pressure on its Latin "good neighbors." To many in Latin America, and perhaps in Canada, the resulting isolation of

Cuba may have been a mistake; it may have forced Castro into such dependence upon the Soviet Union that the installation of Soviet missiles in Cuba eight months later could be directly attributed to it. To Canadians debating potential membership in the OAS, however, the wisdom of the policy was no more instructive than the methods used to achieve it. Today the OAS seems to them merely an instrument through which the U.S. achieves its policy objectives, no matter how dubious and no matter by what means.

The latest and the most telling example of U.S. diplomacy in the hemisphere was the Dominican intervention in April and May of 1965. U.S. policies in the Dominican crisis must, to some degree, have diminished the enthusiasm of the Canadian Government and the Canadian people to join actively in the Inter-American system. The Dominican crisis showed to the Canadians that there is a certain predictable conflict in any crisis between the interests of a regional system and the global interest of the United Nations. It showed that the Organization of American States is not a fully effective instrument which can act with speed and efficiency in an emergency. And, most importantly, it showed that the United States Government, regardless of the need for intervention, did not consider the Organization of American States an institution of a truly collective nature, but rather one which in a crisis would hopefully ratify unilateral U.S. intervention after the fact.

The questions asked in Canada were not unlike the questions asked throughout Latin America. Why was it impossible to seek OAS approval of the intervention before it occurred? At the very least, could not the OAS have been informed before the action was taken—or asked to send observers into Santo Domingo with the United States Marines? President Kennedy was able to secure OAS support for the naval quarantine in the 1962 Cuban missile crisis in less than twenty-four hours. Simply informing the OAS of the United States intention to intervene might not have been a fully satisfactory answer, but it would have provided some evidence of the good intentions of the United States.

Understandably, Latin Americans tend to equate the contemporary U.S. action in the Caribbean with those earlier in the century—intervention broadly resented throughout Latin America. The United States landed sizable contingents of troops in Panama in 1903, in Cuba in 1906, in Mexico in 1914, in Haiti in 1915, and in the Dominican Republic in 1916, and in Nicaragua in 1927. On some occasions the troops remained for many years. But there were fewer U.S. forces used in all these episodes combined than in the Dominican crisis of 1965, when 30,000 U.S. troops were deployed.

And finally the Canadians and Latins alike ask whether the United States had provided ample documentation of the imminent dangers of Communist capture of the Dominican revolution. Others frequently believe that the United States is unduly anxious to ascribe Communist direction to any popular manifestations of the social and economic revolution in which the entire continent is absorbed. It is vital, therefore, for the United States to document with precision the evidence which proves its case in any instance where it either asks for multilateral action or feels it must act alone in the face of Communist efforts in the Hemisphere.

The wavering U.S. definition of collective security and the occasional cavalier U.S. treatment of the Organization of American States and its members lead most Canadians to wonder whether Canadian membership might merely confront their nation with two unpalatable choices: first, to be forced to go along with the United States when it is wrong; or second, to be forced to defy openly the United States.

It is our view, and not ours alone, that U.S. difficulties in Latin America are the very strongest reasons why Canadian membership in the Organization of American States would be invaluable—not invaluable to the United States but to the hemisphere as a whole. An independent Canadian voice within the OAS, speaking for a Canadian Government which is determined to shape its own foreign policy, can be an invaluable source of strength in support of American policies when they are right and in keeping the United States from adopting or promoting policies which are wrong. As a matter of practical power the United States knows that on most occasions it can force the Organization of American States to follow its line or can avoid recourse to the OAS. With a Canada preoccupied in hemisphere relations, with a Canada sitting in the Organization of American States, with a Canada as a potential critic of American policy within the hemisphere, the United States will have to become far more aware and attentive of hemispheric interests.

But more important than Canadian effect on bad U.S. policy judgment, Canadian membership in the Inter-American system could have as great, if not greater, effect than United States membership itself in pursuing those good long-range policies that exist for the hemisphere. The Alliance for Progress is not a bad policy; it is a good policy. But because of Latin American fears of U.S. motivation, the goals of the Alliance are difficult to set, not to speak of achieving them. The progressive forces which have ground to a standstill in Latin America may find much greater encouragement in Canadian prodding than in suspicious U.S. maneuvers.

One Canadian has summed it up succinctly:

As I see it, if Canada undertakes to play its part, there is greater hope that peaceful evolution will gradually solve the chronic ills of Latin America. If we do not, the United States, alone, because of its traditional role and reputation in the hemisphere, might prove as morally and politically incapable of stemming the tide of the violent and autocratic forces of Communism in Latin America in the 'sixties or 'seventies, as it was in China in the 'forties.[6]

Another Canadian has put it even more succinctly:

The argument for Canada's interest in Latin America is that it is in ferment and needs help.

What in all this is the responsibility of the United States? Rather than informing the Canadians that they are remiss in performing their international obligations by failing to join the Organization of American States, the United States should make every effort to build the OAS into an organization of collective security which the Canadians might wish to join.

Many reforms of the OAS are badly needed. Some of them are being promoted now by the Latin governments themselves —and some by the United States.

First, the foreign ministers should be required to meet at least annually and not only under crisis conditions. At present they meet in emergencies or in very infrequent Inter-American Conferences.

Second, the existing Inter-American Peace Committee should be given expanded authority to act to avoid the use of force between members through the peaceful settlement of disputes. At present the Committee, which operates only to moderate between members in dispute, cannot even do this without the approval of both disputing parties. It might be beneficial to make its operations more flexible by permitting its involvement upon the approval of any single member, by encouraging its involvement in situations where disputes can be anticipated, and by providing it a modest operating budget.

Third, a new permanent security committee could be created to act with speed and authority in any instance where elements external to the hemisphere, a dispute between members, or events within any member's territory directly jeopardize the security of the hemisphere. The existing Peace Committee serves only to encourage the peaceful settlements of disputes between two members. There should also be a permanent committee which represents the OAS foreign ministers and which, working in conjunction with the Secretary General, can claim jurisdiction in any crisis which threatens the security of the hemisphere. It could act in advance of a full meeting of the foreign ministers and subsequently could supervise the execution of their decisions. Such a committee might have obviated the U.S. conclusion that the OAS could not have acted with sufficient speed to prevent a calamity in the Dominican Republic.

Fourth, the Secretariat of the OAS should be greatly strengthened in personnel, authority, and function, including the right of the Secretary General to help initiate limited action in the peacekeeping field in advance of the meeting of the foreign ministers. At present the powers of the Secretary General and the Secretariat are extremely limited.

Fifth, a small permanent OAS peacekeeping force should be created for use in disputes between members or, even more important, where elements alien to the hemisphere threaten the security of any member. Such a force would have been ideal in the Dominican crisis. The force would best be fully internationalized and on a stand-by basis under OAS command. The force would be under the ultimate command of the OAS foreign ministers, but the Secretary General and a new Security Committee, under the revised structure described above, might be given the authority to order its limited use where time is of the essence and the foreign ministers had not had the opportunity to meet.

Sixth, long-range OAS reforms should reflect a separation of economic and political issues. A plethora of bureaucratic institutions serves no useful purpose, but the artificial centralization of vastly complex and essentially distinct programs may work to the disadvantage of each. If the decentralization of OAS functions were to come about, it might be possible and desirable to take the centers of OAS economic activities out of Washington and establish the appropriate institutions in Latin America itself.

Separation of the economic and political institutions, with headquarters for the former in Latin America rather than in Washington, might be appropriate encouragement for the first major Canadian step of institutional participation in the economic affairs of the hemisphere.

But the structural and technical OAS reforms are not nearly as important as a new United States attitude toward the organization. The long-term and short-term interests of the United States favor a new national commitment to a strengthened OAS. The relations within the Western Hemisphere in the next

91

two decades will provide a continuing test of the capacity of the United States to lead nations in the throes of social and economic revolution in the preservation of their freedom. The challenge facing the United States is whether it is prepared to welcome the growing independence and political maturity of the developing Latin nations as a new source of strength in the Western world. It must pursue with greater vigor, and with greater attention to the interests of others, long-range policies that will provide for the orderly and progressive growth of the Latin nations. In particular it must pay attention to the establishment of a nuclear-free zone for Latin America and to the eventual internationalization of the Panama Canal under the institutions of the Inter-American system.

Perhaps most important—for Latin America, for the United States, and for Canada—is a greater realization of the purposes of the United States foreign aid through the Alliance for Progress. The purpose of the American foreign aid can only be the development of long-range political stability and independence to allow free peoples to develop according to their own designs. Long-range political stability does not mean authoritarianism. It means the political participation of the people in the free and democratic processes which can produce the development of a society and spread the benefits of development among the people. Foreign aid for too long has been expressed in terms of economic statistics. The task of development might best be expressed not in sterile economic terms, but in terms of people —their awareness of the possible, their education and skills, their determination, and their participation—the impetus they provide and the satisfaction they receive.

If we do not recognize the very real revolution of rising expectations in Latin America—and in Asia and Africa as well— and if we make no effort to guide that revolution in the peaceful course toward political stability and economic prosperity, we will soon have to choose between wars of national liberation everywhere and an illusory isolation in a world where the cause of freedom seems doomed to failure.

If there is an undeniable lesson from the history of Viet Nam, it is that the same thing can happen in any country where the population is susceptible to organization in the pursuit of more progress than the government is providing— where Communist promises have appeal because rising expectations have been inadequately fulfilled. The United States economy and the Western economies collectively cannot afford to fight Viet Nam–type wars everywhere; Western security cannot afford Viet Nam–type wars everywhere. Our only course, therefore, is to attempt to guide the revolution of rising expectations in the knowledge that prosperity, political stability, and political freedom are the surest paths to peace.

The U.S. and Western foreign-aid programs should place new emphasis on the need for the growth of popular participation in the development programs of the developing countries and on the need for increased capacity of the recipient governments to perform effectively in the broad spectrum of development tasks. Western foreign aid must seek to transfer to multilateral management those projects which are essentially economic in nature and do not contribute directly to the growth of political stability or political development.

Consistent with the new emphasis on the administration of and popular participation in development, foreign aid should be made contingent upon a defined set of basic criteria which conduce toward political growth. For example: While we should not insist upon carbon copies of Western political institutions, aid which diminishes or tends to discourage popular participation in government is not justified. No government-to-government aid should be extended to any country whose development plans do not extend to each segment of its population—including the rural peasantry and the modernization of agriculture. No government-to-government aid should be extended to any country where corruption or inefficiency in the government is so widespread that progress is impossible and where no effort is being made to correct it.

The United States and Canada should promote the establishment of a Latin American civil-service academy. They should place new aid concentration on community-development projects including health facilities, housing, schools, libraries, transportation, communications, sewage-disposal facilities, and savings institutions.

Perhaps most important, the two North American countries together can coordinate a vast program to engage the efforts of a private voluntary association of the U.S. and Canadian democracies in a people-to-people aid program so as to encourage the growth and participation by the people of the developing countries in their own development plans. Such a program would encourage business and labor, farm organizations and educational institutions, church groups and professional societies, women's organizations and student groups to undertake their own programs to establish ties with counterpart groups in the developing societies and to encourage their participation in the human infrastructure necessary to achieve and accommodate meaningful progress. The political parties of the North American continent, together, should provide for the establishment of a Latin American institute for democratic development at which representatives of Latin American parties might learn the theoretical and practical aspects of political science.

With the enthusiastic leadership of Canadian provincial governors and American state governors, the subdivisions of the North American federations should seek to establish their own programs for popular participation in development with individual countries in Latin America. In a province- or state-to-country program, with help from Washington and Ottawa, the states and provinces should attempt to enlist the business community, the educational institutions, and the voluntary associations in their own areas in support of coordinated programs to make people-to-people aid projects effective and dramatic.

The essential point in the new approach to foreign aid is found in a comment by Alexis de Tocqueville on the source of the progressive development of nineteenth-century America:

As soon as several of the inhabitants of the United States have taken up an opinion or a feeling which they wish to promote in the world, they look out for mutual assistance; and as soon as they have found one another out, they combine. From that moment they are no longer isolated men, but a power seen from afar, whose actions serve for an example and whose language is listened to.[7]

The development of the North American continent is the result of its democracy—popular democracy—in action. For every cause there is a group. When people want to do things, they get together and promote political action to achieve their ends. From this, development can come; but if development is merely imposed upon a society, it may not come at all—and if it comes, it is unlikely to be shared by the people or to be a source of political stability.

Each American and each Canadian does by instinct what the peoples of Latin America must learn to do if they are to achieve the political and economic stability to secure their independence from external pressure. This is why people-to-people aid programs, centered on political development, must supplement government-to-government programs. The Communist foreign-aid program is not a government-to-government program; it is political organization in the rural and urban areas to channel the energies of the inevitable revolution into the ultimate conquest of an alien ideology. Our challenge is to channel those energies toward a peaceful revolution by which the processes, if not the institutions, of democracy can assure stability to the entire Western Hemisphere.

The United States, because of its history, perhaps because of its power, is suspect in Latin America. It cannot do the job alone. Together the United States and Canada can do the job. That is why, in our judgment, an independent Canada as a full-fledged member of the Inter-American system may be the best guarantor of the security of the entire Western Hemisphere—its own, the Latins', and ours.

One final thought. In May 1966, a separate Office for Relations with Canada was established in the U.S. Department of

95

State under the Bureau of European Affairs. Although this represents progress from the days when Canadian relations were part of the Office of British Commonwealth and Northern European Affairs in the European Bureau, to consider Canada as part of Europe is at least anachronistic. An independent Office of North American Affairs should be created within the Department with an Assistant Secretary in charge. If we truly believe that our relations with Canada are and should be unique, then surely they should no longer be considered part of an irrelevant bureaucratic organization chart. If we desire to encourage Canada to seek its identity within the New World, then we should not treat her as part of the Old.

In World Wars I and II Canada entered the battle to restore peace to Europe long before the United States. But it needed the United States to finish the job. In the Western Hemisphere, the United States has entered the battle to preserve the security of the Latin nations long before Canada. Now it needs Canada to finish the job.

Chapter VI

Two Economies or One?

The realities of U.S. military power are obvious to Canadians and Americans alike. The power of the U.S. economy is far better known in Canada than in the United States.

Military power is an instrument of government—and of government alone. And American military power is as awesome to its own people as to those abroad. But the economic power of the United States is the aggregate of the economic power of all Americans. They are a part of it and therefore tend to be unaware of its equally awesome potential. The Canadians, on the other hand, cannot ignore it.

The economic progress of the North American continent over the next one hundred years, or the next generation, or the next decade, will not be dictated as much by what the economists call the "rationalization factor" of the two economies as by the psychological atmosphere in the two countries.

The United States must learn that economic progress on a continental basis cannot be achieved at the expense of Canadian self-respect—for the Canadians will not allow that to happen. And, as in foreign policy, the Canadians must define a more clear economic identity if the "rationalization" of the two economies is not to mean an American identity for Canada.

Every text and article on U.S.–Canadian economics is so larded with statistics that any commentator is able to find ample proof to support any thesis he may wish to propound. The story of economic relations between the two countries is more a study in psychological patterns than it is of statistics.

Nonetheless the statistics explain why. We will try to group our treatment of them and keep it brief.

It is our preference to be optimistic, so let us look first at the statistics of the opportunity. The combined gross national product of the two North American democracies as of the end of 1965 was $727 billion, or more than $3,000 per person. With the current combined growth rate of approximately 5 per cent per year and a current population growth rate of 1.7 per cent per year, in a generation the continental GNP could be $1,930 billion, or more than $5,700 per person. In a century, the combined GNP could be $95.6 trillion, or more than $77,000 per person. (All figures are in U.S. dollars.)

These figures are misleading because the continental GNP is essentially the American GNP with relatively small Canadian additions. On the other hand, when we talk of the resources of the continent, we recognize how fully continental economic growth depends upon the contributions of both countries. In terms of power for industry, the future of the United States economy and its growth inevitably will continue if not increase its dependence upon Canada—either for uranium to provide nuclear power, or for water to provide more conventional power. In terms of agricultural produce, in terms of raw materials for paper and wood products, in terms of ore and mineral deposits, the strength of the continental economy is inseparable from the resources of Canada.

We have written of a continent whose material progress is so great as to approach a utopia of material satisfaction over the next century. Perhaps in time, either country could achieve that kind of material perfection alone. But reasonable and friendly cooperation, not to speak of "economic rationalization" could assure this continent a century of unbelievable achievement in material terms.

Lest we be smug, the material satisfaction which seems imminent must bring with it the greatest challenge which society has ever faced—the occupation of leisure time for more than leisure. And as the economic growth of our continent continues, it does so at the expense of the "have-not" nations, who despite their own development will, in proportional terms, continue to fall behind the "haves." Again, the opportunity of the continent presents it as well with an obligation. Those who know increasing luxury must find the means to avoid conflict arising from the frustrations of those who are less fortunate.

To dwell on the statistics of opportunity, however, is to avoid the controversy. The real statistics, at least to Canadians, are the statistics of domination—the statistics which show how the United States threatens Canadian economic identity.

The United States gross national product is approximately thirteen times as great as the Canadian GNP.

Over 60 per cent of the Canadian gross national product stems from foreign investment in Canada—and roughly 75 per cent of that foreign investment is American. Thus 45 per cent of the Canadian GNP stems from U.S. investment in Canada—through 6,000 companies owned or controlled by United States interests. United States-controlled companies in Canada amount to a $14-billion investment; in all Europe, the similar figure would be $11.5 billion.

The United States owns more than 60 per cent of the Canadian oil and gas industry, almost 60 per cent of the mining and smelting interests, 35 per cent of the pulp and paper business, 45 per cent of all manufacturing, 25 per cent of the railways, and 13 per cent of the utilities. The United States owns over half the chemical, electrical, and farm-machinery industries in Canada. Foreigners control one of every three Canadian companies with assets over $1 million—and two of every three Canadian firms with assets over $25 million.[1]

Seventy-one per cent of all Canadian imports come from the United States. Fifty-seven per cent of all Canadian exports go to the United States. By comparison, only 22 per cent of U.S. exports go to Canada, and 24 per cent of U.S. imports come from Canada.

With an earlier start in the process of industrialization, the

United States has grown to a position of exporting industrial products to Canada in exchange for raw materials and food-stuffs—the classic relation of a developed economy with an underdeveloped economy—leading perhaps to the classic psychological relations inherent in such a situation.

Canada's population is primarily concentrated within 200 miles of the United States border—a situation that feeds the increasing dominance of the American economy.

It is clear that the Canadian economy has been and will continue to be highly sensitive to the American business cycle, to U.S. business-labor relations, to U.S. wage levels, to U.S. price levels, to the fluctuations on Wall Street. Truly, when the American economy sneezes, Canada catches cold.

The domination of the American economy through trade and investment has an even more telling effect on the Canadian economy than merely prosperity or recession. An economist without sensitivity for national feelings might quite accurately look at the statistics and decide that Canada was merely an adjunct to the U.S. financial and industrial world. The psychological reactions of the Canadian economy may in the long run be disastrous:

> One might say with some degree of truth that Canada as a nation has been afflicted with a sort of branch plant syndrome, with much of our population being content to do just as they do in the States, except for doing it a little worse in quality, somewhat reduced in quantity, and considerably less sophisticated in style.[2]

It is against this statistical background that the current discussion of bilateral or multilateral free trade is taking place. The historical background is also instructive.

Just as Canadian population is smaller, so has its rate of industrialization and economic growth lagged behind that of the United States. The ratio of Canadian to American GNP, both in total and per capita terms has fallen fairly steadily since 1870. So has the ratio of the size of the Canadian to

100

American labor force. So, too, has the ratio of Canadian to American secondary manufacturing. Only in agriculture has the ratio of Canadian to U.S. production risen.

The nineteenth-century history of attempts at economic rationalization and commercial union inevitably became tainted from time to time with the potential, if no real threat, of annexation. In 1911 the experiment was doomed by overanxious American, and oversuspicious Canadian, nationalism.

Cooperation in World War I between the two countries resulted in heavy American investment in Canada. The beginning of a shift in economic relations was thwarted again in 1930, this time by the Smoot-Hawley Tariff, which reduced Canadian trade with the United States by almost 70 per cent in four years. But the Smoot-Hawley Tariff system also gave a great incentive to continued American investment in Canada by permitting American firms with branches in Canada to get the benefit of Canadian materials and prices without a tariff.

World War II cooperation produced a spectacular development of Canadian industry and agriculture and a virtually integrated economy between the two nations. It also produced a Canada dangerously dependent upon the United States, particularly because the war and the postwar sterling crisis closed Canadian trade markets outside North America. Although Canada has tried to build its multilateral trade since the end of World War II, today's domination of the Canadian economy by the United States stems in large part from the extraordinary wartime cooperation between the two countries.

As the gap between the Canadian and American economies has grown, so has Canadian resistance to the idea of reciprocity in trade, which seemed so inviting in the nineteenth century. One hundred years ago, the economies seemed to be roughly identical in nature although the size of the population was not. One hundred years ago, statesmen in both nations saw a potential benefit of two industrializing nations cooperating with each other in their mutual development. But today, no matter how industrialized and developed the Canadian econ-

101

omy may appear to nations in the southern half of the globe, compared with the American economy, it is still undeveloped.

There is, of course, relatively little that the Americans can do about the statistical imbalance of the two countries. It would make little sense to restore the high protective tariffs between the two countries in order to protect Canada from U.S. economic influence. Surely the future for the continent cannot be bright if we resort now to an economic isolationism and autarchy. On the contrary, the prosperity of future years depends upon a greater degree of economic cooperation. That can come, however, only if the Americans realize the extent of their economic power and place realistic restraints upon it. And it can come only if the Canadians are allowed and allow themselves to build an independent economic identity.

Perhaps the major source of friction in the course of American penetration into the Canadian economy is the attitude of many U.S. businessmen in Canada. Understandably, the Canadians tend to generalize on the bad examples set by the few, but Americans cannot console themselves with the fact that the operations of most U.S. subsidiaries and businesses in Canada have been fully exemplary. As is so often the case, the mistakes of the few can create an unhealthy climate for all.

Many an American businessman in Canada tends to act as if he were at home. It is proof of a growing nationalism that Canadians want him to act as if he were a foreign guest—as he is—and as we expect foreigners to act in our own country. Certainly it is quite clear that the obligations upon a foreign investor are quite different from those applicable if he had not gone abroad to invest his money.

In September 1965, the Tupper Report on U.S.–Canadian relations suggested that the Commerce Department in Washington offer guidelines to U.S. businesses in Canada. Included among the recommended guidelines:

1. Public shares in the ownership of U.S. subsidaries in Canada should be offered to Canadian citizens.

2. U.S. subsidaries in Canada should retain the services of Canadian directors.

3. To the degree possible, Canadian managerial talent should be employed in the operations of U.S. business in Canada.

4. The United States personnel selected to operate U.S. business concerns in Canada should be chosen for their capacity to adapt to the Canadian environment and should make a sincere effort to participate in Canadian community affairs.

5. U.S. business operations in Canada should buy their components and services, when available at competitive prices, from Canadian rather than American sources.

6. U.S. subsidiaries in Canada should make every reasonable effort to export their products as well as to sell to the domestic Canadian market.

7. Whenever economically feasible, U.S. businesses in Canada should develop research facilities in Canada rather than relying on their U.S. parent companies to meet their research needs, a practice which contributes to the "brain drain" of some of Canada's most promising engineering and scientific talent.

8. U.S. companies in Canada with fifty or more Canadian shareholders should publish annual financial statements, rather than permitting their records to be reported only as part of the parent company.

On March 31, 1966, the Canadian Minister of Trade and Commerce, Robert H. Winters, sent the Canadians' own list of similar guidelines to major American subsidiaries and American-owned businesses in Canada. Of course, the Canadian Government has the responsibility to indicate what it expects of foreign investors in its country. But it is even more important for the future that the American Government recognize its responsibilities to indicate what it expects of its foreign investors abroad. The future relations of the two economies—their capacity to take advantage of the unparalleled opportunity that lies before them to build a miraculous and universal prosperity on the North American continent—depend upon an American awareness of the need for restraint in the exercise of its economic power.

It is of course contrary to traditional nationalism and to conventional wisdom for a nation to be extraordinarily sensitive to the concerns of others. But to a great degree, it is the purpose of this book to express to its American readers that unless they understand and are more sensitive to Canadian nationalism, the future of U.S.–Canadian economic, political, and military cooperation is not a bright one.

What we ask of American business in Canada is no more than what it increasingly practices in other parts of the world. Returning to an earlier theme, because Americans are so unaware of the independent status of Canada—of the differences between Americans and Canadians—American businessmen do not think of a business operation in Canada with the same caution or care that they think of a business operation in Latin America, Africa, or Asia. In those far-off lands, where the national differences are obvious, it is only good business to be aware of local sensitivities and to shape the course of one's business operations to take account of potential adverse reactions. Perhaps it is the threat of nationalization, perhaps it is the personal apprehension of living in a foreign land where customs and language and dress are so different, perhaps it is the awareness that the American Government is directly concerned to see that business operations do not jeopardize foreign-policy interests. Whatever the reason, it is obvious that American business in almost every country in the world has become increasingly sensitive to local concerns and customs.

The best example is the training given to most American businessmen before they go abroad. The U.S. business community has broadly accepted the responsibility of assuring that its employees sent abroad are given some education in the politics, history, culture, and economy of the foreign countries to which they are assigned. This has been true, for example, in U.S. business operations in the Middle East and Latin America. Unfortunately, it has not been true of U.S. businessmen sent to Canada.

There are some seminars available for U.S. executives on their way to business in Canada—such as the programs at Goddard College, in Vermont, and at Cornell University, in New York. But in view of the vast numbers of U.S. businessmen in Canada, those programs are much too small. A brief, privately endowed seminar, enthusiastically encouraged and aided by the expertise of the appropriate agencies of the U.S. administration, could do much to avoid misunderstanding and apprehension when U.S. business representatives take up their posts in Canada.

Again it is well to remind Canadians and Americans alike that it takes only a few companies, only a relatively small number of businessmen, to seriously jeopardize the future of continental cooperation. Neither the Canadians nor the Americans should allow the few to shape the future.

The problem raised by the activities of American businessmen is matched by an equally serious problem raised by the policies of the United States Government. It is quite natural for a government to try to extend its policies over its citizens when they are abroad, but, because the American involvement in the Canadian economy is so immense, when the United States extends its policies across the Canadian frontier to affect U.S. business, it also has an extraordinary impact on Canadian national life.

We cite two examples: U.S. policy to correct its balance of payments; U.S. policy on trade with the Communist countries. The differences between the two areas are important and might be better understood in Washington and Ottawa.

After a reluctance to do so, the United States in late 1965 began to apply restrictions against U.S. investment in Canada similar to those it has applied against U.S. investment elsewhere in order to overcome its serious balance-of-payments deficit. It was forced to do so. When it exempted investment in Canada from the earlier regulations, it had encouraged a significant growth in U.S. investment in Canada, which in turn meant that a large measure of the progress made in the U.S. balance of payments elsewhere was counteracted by an increased outflow of capital to Canada.

The Canadian resentment and outcry was extraordinary. The inevitable result of the U.S. balance-of-payments policy was, they were sure, a serious contraction in the Canadian economy and the sudden impairment of Canada's own balance-of-payments problem.

It is again imperative for the Canadians to understand the responsibilities imposed by world leadership upon the United States. The United States balance-of-payments crisis is not simply the case of a country running into some difficulty and therefore having to make some sacrifices in order to restore economic balance. The stability of the entire international financial structure created after World War II rests on the stability of the American dollar and its acceptability as an international reserve currency. Each dollar of the American balance-of-payments deficit is a dollar in foreign hands as a claim against U.S. gold supplies. We are at a stage in international finances where the number of dollars held abroad as reserves has reached the saturation point—where additional dollars in large numbers might conceivably cause a serious run on U.S. gold and serious instability in international finances.

It is all very well to say that this crisis is an indication of the need for reform in the international monetary system. It is. But the countries of Europe, quite correctly, will not permit substantive reform in the international monetary system if it simply allows the United States to maintain an enormous deficit. Europe has insisted that the United States balance its international payments first—and the United States has no alternative.

A world economic crisis of catastrophic proportions will result if the United States is not soon able to get its balance-of-payments problem under control. This was the reason for the U.S. administration balance-of-payments guidelines to American investors in Canada. And despite the harsh consequences to the Canadian economy, Canada has a vital stake in the success of the American effort. In fact, because of the American penetration of the Canadian economy, the Canadian interest in the success of American payments policy is greater than that of any other nation.

U.S. trade policy with the Communist countries, as it is extended to American subsidiaries and American-owned compa-

106

nies in Canada, is a completely different matter. Even though it is not the policy of the United States Government to trade broadly with Communist countries, it would not cause a crisis in international relations nor would it severely jeopardize American foreign policy if American companies in Canada were to conduct such trade on a broader basis than those in the United States.

We do not advocate violation of the United States Trading with the Enemy Act, but neither do we think it a wise course for the United States to apply the provisions of that act stringently against American-owned companies in Canada at the expense of U.S.–Canadian harmony.

It is clear that Canadian trade policy is different from American trade policy. It is clear that the growth of Canadian trade has been limited because American-owned companies in Canada have felt constrained to abide by United States trading policies and not to entertain the opportunity to sell to Communist countries. American-owned flour mills in Canada, for example, have refused to take part in the sale of Canadian flour to Cuba. United States subsidiaries have refused to sell fertilizer, newsprint, and farm machinery to Communist China.

Both the Merchant-Heeney Report of June 1965 and the Tupper Report of September 1965 suggested examination by the two governments of some means by which "this irritant to our relationship may be removed, without encouraging the evasion of United States law by citizens of the United States."[3]

It surely must not be the policy of either government to encourage, or appear to permit, the flow of U.S. business investment into Canada in order to participate in trade which U.S. law forbids. But the U.S. Government, the U.S. business community, and the U.S. people must realize that foreign investment is a privilege—and because the Canadian economy requires heavy emphasis on the development of export markets, foreign investment in Canada must eventually be limited unless it is free to cooperate with Canadian policy. The issues are difficult, and a satisfactory solution will be complicated, but the responsibility of the U.S. Government to act effectively is clear.

Let the essential point be understood. Canada and the Canadians are undertaking a search for objectives in foreign policy, for a national identity—and unless the United States is very careful, that economic identity will be built as well around the principle of anti-Americanism. If we wish to build on the North American continent a model for relations between independent nations, then the United States must be more attentive and more aware both of Canadian concerns and of the disasters that can stem from the careless application of power—military or economic.

The economic nationalism growing in Canada is an anti-American nationalism. Recently a professor at an American university suggested that U.S. corporations establishing subsidiaries in Canada should be required to divest themselves of ownership at the end of twenty-five years. This kind of proposal finds emotional support in Canada, not because of the statistics of American economic domination, but because of the fact that Americans tend to be so insensitive to Canadian fears. The progressive answer for the Canadians is surely not to end American investment in Canada. The progressive answer for the Canadians can only be supplied by the United States—a more conscious effort to become aware of its impact.

It is within this framework that the next decade, generation, or century can see the "rationalization of the two economies"— the growth of economic cooperation on the North American continent to match the political cooperation necessary to build a model of relations between independent nations.

It is almost impossible to overestimate the importance of the 1965 U.S.–Canadian agreement on tariff reductions on automobiles and automotive parts. It, like the free trade in agricultural machinery which has existed for twenty years, is a clear example of international economic progress where the national economic interests converge. The directions which the two governments will now take must await not only authoritative interpretation of the results of the automotive-parts agreement but also a detailed study by each government of the economic ramifications of any further steps proposed.

108

The initial indications are that the automotive agreement has been an enormous success. Despite the hearings on auto safety, Canada's automobile production in 1966 ran well above 1965. Canadian exports of cars to the United States increased fourfold in one year. Canadian employment in the field has risen dramatically.

The purpose of the pact, from the Canadian standpoint, was the rapid stimulation of Canadian industrial development. From the United States standpoint, other than the fact that the pact was favored by the major automobile producers, the reasons for the automotive agreement may have seemed more obscure. But by giving impetus to Canadian industrial development, the United States was encouraging a Canadian economic identity not built on anti-Americanism but on the visible virtue of U.S.–Canadian economic cooperation.

And perhaps most important of all, to both countries, the automotive agreement was a small step which could provide some measure of the economic benefits or dangers to either from greater cooperation in a free-trade atmosphere.

Eighty-five years ago, the poet Walt Whitman wrote in his "Specimen Days":

Some of the more liberal of the presses here are discussing the question of a Zollverein between the United States and Canada. It is proposed to form a union for commercial purposes—to altogether abolish the frontier tariff line, with its double sets of custom house officials now existing between the two countries, and to agree upon one tariff for both, the proceeds of this tariff to be divided between the two governments on the basis of population. It is said that a large proportion of the merchants of Canada are in favor of this step, as they believe it will materially add to the business of the country, by removing the restrictions that now exist on trade between Canada and the United States. Those persons who are opposed to the measure believe that it would increase the material welfare of the country, but it would loosen the bonds between Canada and England; and this sentiment overrides the desire for commercial prosperity. Whether the sentiment can continue to bear the strain put upon it is a question. It is thought by many that commercial considerations must in the end prevail.

The debate still continues. In a 1964 public-opinion survey, 65 per cent of all Canadians were reported to favor economic union with the United States. Broken down: 79 per cent of the unemployed, 78 per cent of the students, 78 per cent of Quebec, and 75 per cent of the Maritime Provinces were reported to favor economic union with the United States.[4] But still the hesitancy exists, not because as Whitman wrote "it would loosen the bonds between Canada and England" but because it might destroy the opportunity for a separate Canadian identity.

If greater economic cooperation between the United States and Canada is to come, who will take part? A bilateral free-trade area would require extraordinary American business restraint if Canada is to retain its economic identity. There are many Canadians who believe that free trade between Canada and the United States is possible, from the Canadian standpoint, only if it is accompanied by free trade with other countries as well, so that Canada will have an opportunity to expand other foreign investment in her own country and to expand her foreign markets outside the United States. We are not economists, but as those familiar with the political process, we are impressed by the logic which says that Canada can only participate in partnership with the United States if it is not totally dependent and dominated by the United States.

A bilateral free-trade area is an unknown quantity. Canadians may fear that it may remove their flexibility, their mobility, their opportunity for independence. If multilateral association is a better guarantor of Canadian identity—if U.S.–Canadian–British free trade is a safer course—if U.S.–Canadian ties with the European Free Trade Area would be more suited to Canadian concerns—then bilateralism should be set aside. We do not believe that bilateral free trade is sinister; neither do we believe that there is anything holy about it.

110

If greater economic cooperation between Canada and the United States is to come, how comprehensive will it be? While we do not shy away from bold steps, the brash brush-stroke treatment is typically American. Bold and sudden free trade between Canada and the United States may fail merely by reinforcing Canadian suspicions and caution. Some argue that a more sure course might be to build one block upon another. North American relations are already fragile.

A comprehensive free-trade agreement is bound to be either an immense success or an immense failure. Such an agreement would be premature without Canadian confidence in it. If the automotive agreement proves successful, perhaps other steps could be taken quickly. Surely the exploration of similar agreements in aircraft parts, or chemicals, or fertilizers would be worth while. Let progress come, and let it come quickly—but we need not risk all by a dramatic step that would contribute to, rather than calm, Canadian fears.

If greater United States–Canadian economic cooperation is to come, when will it come? The directions which the two governments will now take must await not only authoritative interpretation of the results of the automotive-parts agreement, but also detailed study by each government of the economic ramifications of any further steps proposed. Only the confidence gained by experience will lead the nations to the realization that greater free trade is possible or impossible. Each country must have more and better information than it now has. That information can come of course from hypothetical studies, and they must be undertaken. But the reliable information on which to act is the information which stems from experience.

If both countries wait until both are certain that all trade barriers can be lowered at once, then both countries may wait forever. The goal is greater confidence: and confidence is built by small steps taken on solid ground.

We envisage on the North American continent a model of relations between independent nations. It will not happen overnight—and if we try to make it happen overnight, it may not happen at all. Still we must get on with the job.

Chapter VII

Water: The Politics of Supply and Demand

The Tupper Report, issued by eleven U.S. House Members, in September 1965, was the product of intensive research and an elaborate effort to make a helpful contribution to the U.S.–Canadian dialogue which would be well received in both Canada and the United States. By and large it was, with significant editorial endorsement from many of the major Canadian newspapers.

An editorial in the Toronto *Globe and Mail,* however, demonstrated just how difficult it is to overcome Canadian suspicions of American motives:

> Still and all and despite a good many other kind words from the 11, we cannot help wondering if they would have bothered making Canadians feel so pleasantly important if they had not been deeply concerned about a matter that really is important to the United States—all that fresh water that is running out of Canadian rivers into the Atlantic and the Pacific when it might just as well, reason the 11, be diverted to quenching the U.S. thirst.[1]

This book and every other text on its subject inevitably describe at length the imbalance of military and economic power that dominates the U.S.–Canadian relationship. We have argued the case that for all its military power, the deterrence of a nuclear attack on the United States depends upon the twenty minutes' time that Canadian cooperation through NORAD and the DEW line provides. Similarly, American economic power depends at least in part upon the natural mineral resources and raw materials of an abundant Canada. But no one would argue that the United States in either of these fields feels utterly dependent upon Canada. It is not obvious to most Americans.

Water is different. It is the area in which Canada holds a trump card, and the United States knows that it does. It is the area in which Canada has the opportunity to exercise extraordinary leverage in the course of future U.S.–Canadian relations.

Of all the abundance of an abundant land, no statistic is more startling than the fact that Canada has 35 per cent of all the fresh water in the world. And of all the domestic problems in the United States, none is becoming more severe than the shortage of "cool, clear water."

The only aspect of the American problem which directly involves the Canadians as well is Great Lakes water.

The St. Lawrence Seaway was conceived as an extraordinary boon to the economy of both countries—and it has been. It is today severely threatened by pollution and declining water levels in the Great Lakes.

Pollution, particularly in Lake Erie, threatens the health and safety of all those who use it or its water, Americans and Canadians alike. It is beginning to have a significant effect on the fish population of the lake, which cannot live because it is too dirty. Man-made sewage in Lake Michigan is accelerating at such a rate that weed expansion threatens to clog the middle of the lake in years to come. Shipping through the lakes is in danger.

The causes of pollution in the Great Lakes are known— although no obviously feasible solution has yet been discovered.

On the other hand, the experts do not even know the causes of the lake level problems. As this book is written, Great Lakes water levels seem to be adequate. Six months earlier they were not—and the reason for their rise is as unknown as was the reason for their fall.

What is known, however, is that there is insufficient water in the Great Lakes, even if it could be depolluted, to use for diversion purposes either in the United States or Canada. The Chairman of the U.S.–Canadian Ninth Conference on Great Lakes Research recently suggested that the Great Lakes could provide water for consumption, recreation, and navigation of one hundred times the population now located in the lands surrounding the lakes—but because of poor management, the lakes today can barely support the current 50 million population in the area.[2]

At the same conference a U.S. official was quoted as saying:

These great inland seas are beginning to fail mankind. We have been misusing them to the point that they can no longer serve us as in the past.

Our use of the water needs to be managed. The challenge is that of soaring population, shrinking allotment of space per person and gathering storms of conflict over stretching natural resources . . .

All these signs are those of the healthy America of our dreams—until we go to swim in or drink some of the water. The realization came years ago that pollution was getting out of hand.[3]

The state of the Great Lakes is a continental water problem. But it is merely a small part of an increasingly severe United States water problem. The water problem in the United States is shortage—in the East, shortage of purified water; in the West, shortage of water, period. The Northeast Coast of the United States since 1960 has faced the worst drought in 80 years. Over 1,000 United States communities in 1965 had to place severe restrictions on the use of water. A dairy in New Jersey sold artesian well water at more than 16¢ a quart.

The water available to the Eastern sections of the United States is plentiful but its quality is exceptionally low.

Some rivers in that area, as in others, which start out as runoff from mountain springs of the purest and tastiest water, end up as foul and filthy liquid which must undergo extensive chemical treatment before it can be made fit for consumption. An example of this is the Hudson River in New York state which someone has aptly described as a poisoned water hole.[4]

Expanded diversion of Great Lakes waters to serve the needs of the Eastern seaboard of the United States would seem a natural solution. But under present conditions, it simply is not possible. Great Lakes water levels are already threatened, and Great Lakes pollution already exists.

However severe the Eastern water problem is in the United States, the Western water problem is far worse. The Western states simply do not have water—and they must have vast amounts for irrigation, for the very existence of many of their communities. The Boise Valley in Idaho, the Yakima Valley in Washington, the Central Valley of California, the Phoenix area in Arizona, the Salt Lake City environs in Utah, and the Rio Grande Valley development in Colorado, New Mexico, and Texas all owe their very life to extraordinary irrigation projects.

The supply-and-demand statistics of water in the United States tell the story simply. The total stream flow of fresh water in the United States was measured in 1954 at approximately 1,100 billion gallons a day. In 1954, the United States used 300 billion gallons a day, or 27 per cent of its stream flow. It is estimated that in 1980 the United States will require 559 billion gallons a day, or 51 per cent of its stream flow. In the year 2000, it is estimated that the United States will use 888 billion gallons a day, or 81 per cent of its stream flow.[5] And in the 21st century, as the population continues to expand, the problem will become increasingly serious.

The statistics are not, in fact, as bad as they seem, for much of the water used in the United States or anywhere is simply "withdrawn" and can be returned to the stream and reused many times, as long as the necessary steps are taken to maintain its quality. For example, while 60 per cent of the water drawn off for irrigation purposes is actually consumed, or lost to the water supply, fully 99 per cent of the water diverted for steam-electric power cooling can be continually reused if kept under appropriate quality control.

Thus the estimates of consumptive water uses, of water that once used is gone forever from the supply, show that 10 per cent of the stream flow was lost in 1954, 11 per cent would be lost in 1980 and about 14 per cent in 2000. But these figures too are misleading, for they assume an extraordinary capacity for pollution control and conservation. In the most comprehensive study undertaken of the nation's water needs, a U.S. Senate Subcommittee in 1961 reported that the nation, under minimum flow requirements, would be using 49 per cent of its total water resources in 1980 and 63 per cent in the year 2000.[6]

In many other problems faced by industrialized-urbanized society, the solution comes through substitution or synthetics. When a fiber is inadequate to do a job, the chemists invent a new one. When ground space is unavailable, the engineers have built into the skies. When time is of the essence, the scientists have developed ever more rapid modes of communication. But, except in drink, we have developed no substitute for water.

The National Water Institute in the United States has estimated that the country uses 2,675 gallons every day for each American. He drinks and eats only about 2 gallons. He requires 58 more gallons a day in his home. The farmer uses 766 gallons a day per consumer to grow food. The utilities and industrial companies use 849 gallons a day per American.[7]

As President Kennedy said: "Anybody who can solve the problem of water will be worthy of two Nobel Prizes—one for peace and one for science."[8]

What are the solutions? There are four potential areas of solution: desalination; antipollution control; a far more serious and comprehensive effort to control the flow of existing U.S. water; and reliance on water from Canada.

Ninety per cent of the world's water is salty, and although ships on the high seas have been desalting ocean waters for six centuries, the process is still prohibitively expensive for mass production of usable water. The production cost today is ap-

116

proximately $1.00 per 1,000 gallons. If all U.S. water used cost that amount, the U.S. would be spending over $300 million a day for water. This is not to say that the production costs will not come down—nor is it to say that desalination, even at present costs, cannot help to meet pressing water shortages. And it certainly is not to say that research in the processes of desalination should not continue.

One cannot view the march of science over the last fifty years without concluding that it is quite probable that a desalination process will eventually be developed, by which water from the oceans can be made available as cheaply as water from the streams. But that is in the future—perhaps a long way into the future. Desalinized water today can serve emergency needs, such as the Guantánamo Naval Base, cut off by Castro from Cuba's fresh water, and the Kuwait oil fields. And it may begin to serve in a small way the problems of our cities, as through the new giant desalination plant planned for Long Island, New York. But the process has not progressed to the point where we can now rely upon it as a source of water in the amounts which the United States will increasingly need.

Antipollution is, of course, one part of any solution. And the United States has failed to undertake as comprehensive and vigorous a program of antipollution as it can and as it must. But no one should expect that the full answer lies in antipollution or pollution control. For the demands of the U.S. water supply are such that over the next hundred years, even assuming complete quality control of all of its fresh water, the United States must either find new sources or undertake extraordinary cutbacks in water utilization.

Similarly, better U.S. control of the flow of its waters would help in its water shortages immeasurably, but would not solve them. It is obvious when various parts of the country suffer from perennial floods and others from perennial drought that proper utilization of the water supply in the United States could help. But we cannot ignore the immensity of the problem that will confront this nation in fifty years' time if we do not plan now not just to maximize control over existing water flows and supplies in the United States, but to make plans to expand those supplies in some meaningful way.

It is the immensity of the long-range problem which makes Canada's vast supply of water so inviting to the United States. Short of an incredible technological breakthrough in the processing of sea water at acceptable costs, there may be no reasonable alternative for the expansion of U.S. water supplies compatible with its needs than the long-range development of a continental water-sharing plan.

The Government of Canada should not, and the Government of the United States should not ask it to, consider making available to the United States water supplies which it needs for its own purposes. But if the estimates of abundance are accurate there would seem to be no serious obstacle to the development of a continental plan for developing water resources that can meet the needs of both nations.

We believe that the Canadian Government would be remiss in its duties to its own citizens if before entering into any continental water-sharing plan it did not assure itself that its water resources for the "second hundred years" could easily be met by waters not available to the United States. And to assure that U.S. water reliance on Canada is kept within reasonable bounds, Canada would be justified in insisting that the United States make a better effort to control its own water resources before beginning to rely on those of another country.

The United States in its turn has a responsibility to its own citizens, and to Canada as well, to seek a far more comprehensive solution to the control of water supplies and quality in the United States before it asks for outside help. Americans and their government have been too cavalier in their attitude toward the future in their utilization of the water already at their command. A continental water-sharing program must not simply give them a continued excuse to waste water. It is all too easy to view the Canadian abundance of water and conclude that we need not take harsh steps of resource and pollution control. But there may well come the day when the continental water resources may themselves prove inadequate for

118

the continent's needs. And the early political reality may be that a continental water-sharing program, which is impossible without Canadian cooperation, can come only after the United States has proven to its neighbor that it is willing to take the steps necessary to make the best use of its own water resources before it relies on Canadian generosity.

What should the United States do? We have written of the increasingly anachronistic nature of state government in the American federation. Nowhere is this more clear than in the area of water resources. The Merchant-Heeney Report noted:

> Primary responsibility for moving ahead, and much of the expertise, particularly in electricity, rests with the system owners—public and private—in the two countries. And much of the authority rests elsewhere, notably within State and Provincial jurisdiction.[9]

This is a severe problem not just between the two countries, but within the two countries. The American states, particularly in the northeastern quadrant, do not have sufficient jurisdiction to meet the problem of water resources control alone. The water supplies for all the American states are spread over a number of different states and a number of jurisdictions. To the degree that major rivers are utilized as state boundaries, the jurisdictional problems are even more intense.

Water control in the United States must be either the business of the federal government or the business of regional associations of states set up specifically for this problem. The development of interstate authorities with sufficient power to act effectively has been painfully slow. The federal government's approach has been equally inadequate.

The American governments, both federal and state, have not been inactive. A 1964 Senate report cited 3,151 water-resources projects underway, or contemplated, at a total cost of $60 billion. In 1965, the federal government took an important step in the creation of the Water Resources Council to coordinate the work of the federal agencies. And it provided for the formation of river-basin commissions through interstate compact.

But the tough and comprehensive decisions have yet to be made. For example, antipollution efforts in the United States seem to be centered on the control of pollution—the purifying of water once polluted—rather than on ending pollution. It is imperative to devise the scientific means by which polluted waters can be made pure simply and inexpensively; it is all the more necessary to devise the means which will end the original pollution of water. This requires new means of waste disposal, hopefully not merely to substitute the pollution of air for the pollution of water. And it requires penalties for those who pollute the waters. One current approach considered essential to the antipollution effort is tax benefits to industries who undertake research programs in how to get rid of their waste without polluting the air or water resources. Perhaps we have reached the stage, however, when it would be even more appropriate to apply a pollution tax to those who contribute to the depurification of water—whether they be private individuals, corporations, or government entities.

Recently the five U.S. states of Michigan, Indiana, Ohio, Pennsylvania, and New York reached an important new agreement with the federal government to meet the pollution problem in Lake Erie. This is a welcome step, but without the continued priority emphasis of the federal government, the steps taken thus far will be insufficient even to contain the growth of pollution, much less to reverse the trend.

The United States approach to the control of its river flow is also inadequate. Without bold new departures and grand schemes to divert wasteful into productive flow, the United States will not be fully justified in seeking reliance upon Canada for greatly expanded water resources. For example, the costs of a mammoth project of diverting the excess waters of the rivers which find their beginnings in Wisconsin, Minnesota, and the northern Plains States into the Great Lakes would be small indeed compared with the costs of the perennial floods through the Mississippi and Missouri River valleys, which these excess waters cause—and small compared to the costs of a rapid decline in the levels of the Great Lakes. This is a program which requires national leadership; it is too great for any locality or state to undertake or even to comprehend. It would be a unique contribution to the common interests of Canada and the United States, while at the same time serving to make more secure the lives of those who have chosen as their home the river valleys of the Mississippi and the Missouri.

Also, the desalination experimentation program of the federal government is too small. Immediate crises so overwhelm those responsible for the exercise of government that long-range crises are often ignored. The water shortage that will be imposed upon the United States over the next two generations may well in fact become the most severe domestic crisis this nation has ever faced. A cheap process of desalination is one potential answer, and it must be pursued with the impetus which only federal government demands can provide.

Finally the United States must refrain from independent forays into water diversion that merely complicate U.S.–Canadian relations. If for no other reason, political common sense dictates that the United States cannot expect full cooperation from the Canadian Government in a continental water-sharing program if it does not constantly demonstrate by its own actions that it is genuinely willing to cooperate. Programs for the diversion of further waters out of the Great Lakes without consultation with the Canadian Government would be irresponsible—in terms of international interests and U.S. national interest alike. They make far more difficult the painstaking negotiations with the Canadian Government for the development of a continental water-sharing plan by demonstrating a hypocrisy which many Canadians suspect attends all U.S. policies.

What are the Canadian responsibilities? Americans are in a poor position to argue the moral responsibilities toward a neighbor in need. Cavalier treatment of Canadian interests has not provided a particularly receptive Canadian ear to such an American argument. Nonetheless the U.S. need is real now and will increasingly be so.

Canadian Resource Minister Arthur Laing has said: "This is our water and we will do with it what we want . . . As far as water is concerned it is not negotiable." [10] Certainly, from a Canadian standpoint, their water must remain nonnegotiable until they know how much they have and how much they could spare if they were disposed to do so. In August of 1965 the Canadian and Ontario Governments agreed to survey whether waters now flowing into Hudson Bay might be diverted southward. The study was estimated to take five years. The Ontario Water Resources Commission has estimated that it would take between ten to fifteen years to study Canada's northern rivers and determine the abundance of water and the possibility of diversion. Elsewhere it has been estimated that it will take more than fifty years to complete an initial survey of Canada's waters, to analyze tides, flows, water levels, etc.[11]

At least one Canadian legislator has suggested that the survey time claimed by the Canadian Government is "ridiculous." [12] He and others are concerned that the United States may unilaterally divert such great amounts of water from the Great Lakes that, unless Canada gets on with its own job of diverting waters into the Great Lakes, shipping through the St. Lawrence Seaway will come to a standstill.

Without a Canadian survey of its water, discussions of a continental water-sharing program cannot be made. And perhaps more relevant to Canada, without surveying its own water resources it cannot consider realistically a nationwide development program utilizing the water resources at its command.

Unfortunately, up to this point, continental water-sharing programs have been viewed in Canada only from the perspective of how much benefit the United States would receive. It might be appropriate to concentrate briefly on the value of Canadian water development to Canada.

New water into the Great Lakes maintains or increases the capacity of the lakes and St. Lawrence Seaway system to encourage shipping into the heartland of both countries. Water-development schemes in Canada could bring economic development to areas of the country which are now only sparsely settled.

Canada surely does not intend, nor should the United States

ask, that Canadian water be supplied gratis to the United States. Quite the contrary, to the degree that it is a resource which the United States desperately needs, its sale by the Canadians could be a significant source of revenue to the country.

Finally, the development of Canadian water resources in an integrated national or continental program could provide the Canadian Government with an extraordinary lever in its relations with the United States—and in future years the leverage will increase.

One example of such a plan was proposed by T. W. Kierans in March 1960. The basic theory of the Kierans plan was that "the concept of the Great Lakes as a prime source of water should be revised and that they should be in fact considered as a huge reservoir area capable of substantial and continuous replenishment by at least 25,000 cubic feet per second from the vast and little used James Bay Watershed. This new water added to the Great Lakes would then be sold from the Great Lakes reservoir to users under Joint International Control." [13]

Kierans suggested that fresh water be collected from the rivers which converge into the James Bay, pumped up to the plateau of the Great Northern Clay Belt, passed down the Harricanaw River bed, which would be widened for the purpose, through a connection to the headwaters of the Ottawa River to Lake Temiskaming, then on to Lake Nipissing and finally via the French River into Georgian Bay on Lake Huron. The total cost, including reversal of the Harricanaw River, numerous power plants, locks and channel widening, would be $2 billion plus interest. He estimates eventual revenue at $19 million per year.

An even more incredible scheme is that of the North American Water and Power Alliance. It is a truly continental approach to water resources. Its description is staggering:

> Of an average annual drainage area runoff of 663,000,000 acre feet of water, approximately 110,000,000 acre feet would be utilized.
> A series of dams and power stations in Alaska and northern British Columbia would collect water and pro-

vide power to pump water up to the Rocky Mountain
Trench Reservoir in southeastern British Columbia. From
the Rocky Mountain Trench Reservoir, water would be
pump-lifted to the Sawtooth Reservoir in Central Idaho.
From there, water would gravity-flow to the western
states. Outflow from the north end of the Rocky Mountain Trench Reservoir, augmented by 48,000,000 acre feet
per year of unused eastern slope runoff, would supply the
Great Lakes Complex via the Canadian-Great Lakes
Waterway which would cross Canada linking the Pacific
Ocean with the Great Lakes-St. Lawrence Complex. The
NAWAPA concept would also include a system of inter-
connecting waterways which would tie the eastern land
mass of Canada to the Great Lakes Complex.

Total power generation would be 100,000,000 kilowatts per year. Of this amount, approximately 70,000,000
kilowatts per year would be available for marketing.
Pumping requirements would consume 30,000,000 kilowatts per year of NAWAPA-generated power.

Estimated construction costs, based on 1964 prices, are
$100 billion. About 20 years would be required to com-
plete the project after resolution of political and international considerations.[14]

NAWAPA would provide 22 million acre feet of water annually for industrial, municipal, and agricultural uses in Canada; for the same purposes it would provide 78 million acre
feet of water to the United States, and 20 million acre feet of
water to Mexico. It would provide 30 million kilowatts of
power for sale in Canada, 38 million kilowatts of power for
sale in the United States, and 2 million kilowatts of power for
sale in Mexico. It would stabilize and control water levels on
the Great Lakes. It would provide seaways from the Great
Lakes to Alberta and to James Bay, between Hudson Bay and
Lake Superior. The Canadian national income from agriculture, livestock, mining, and manufacturing is estimated to be
subject to a $9-billion annual increase through NAWAPA; the

124

United States would gain a $30 billion increase in the same areas.

NAWAPA is a concept. It has not been laid out in specific detail. It is surely not the only way to approach the continent's water problems. On the contrary, it is merely an idea—a dream.

It would be hopelessly shortsighted of the United States not to be interested in examining all proposals made for continental water-sharing. Its interests are obvious.

It would in our view be shortsighted of Canada and Canadians as well to ignore thinking about continental programs of water development—either for sharing with the United States or for their own development. The growth of the Canadian nation has in large measure been dominated by the fact that the great bulk of the Canadian people live within 200 miles of the United States border. Trade and transportation ties run north and south across the border more than east and west across the nation.

If the French explorer Pierre la Verendrye had discovered a river route across the prairies to the Pacific in his travels of more than two hundred years ago, Canada could be a more united nation today. If the transportation system of Canada, if the power system of Canada, if the economic-development potential of Canada traced a route from east to west and back again, the provinces could be united as never before and Canadian nationhood and identity could be made ever more firm. From an American standpoint, perhaps Canadian growth would merely be a by-product of continental water development. To the Canadian, the fact that the United States can share in the abundance of Canadian water could be merely the by-product of a Canadian design to develop its own economy and its own nationhood.

The nations of the North American continent must seek to avoid the national enmities which can grow out of unilateral decisions to divert waters from their joint uses. From the beginning of history man has fought his fellow man over the use of and the right to water. In nineteenth-century America, the

125

pioneers in the West fought and killed each other in senseless arguments over the right to water. Today in the Middle East, the diversion of a river is the source of a possible war.

Surely the United States and Canada can be more responsible than those who have gone before. Surely these two nations, to whom the world looks for a model of international relations, can learn from the folly of others. We believe that the two nations should negotiate a treaty on water diversion, that would on the one hand bind the United States not to divert necessary waters from the Great Lakes and in exchange would assure Canadian participation in a joint program to supply sufficient waters to the Great Lakes to allow the concept of the St. Lawrence Seaway economy to take shape. As a Canadian member of Parliament has described the effect of such a treaty:

> No longer could the U.S. "pull the plug" at Chicago. More water from the Great Lakes, in other words, must not be allowed to flow down the Mississippi. These commitments to behave in a predictable way are essential. They will also have to be forthcoming before Canada agrees to turn on the taps from the North.[15]

A treaty on water diversion; a comprehensive effort by the United States to pursue research in desalination; a comprehensive U.S. program of pollution control; a real U.S. effort at adequate control of the flow of its own excess waters; diversion of excess U.S. river waters into the Great Lakes; an intensive Canadian study of the abundance of its water resources and needs—with all these the continent may be ready to consider continental water development.

The place to undertake such consideration is the International Joint Commission.

Chapter VIII

The Continental Institutions

International relations most often bring to mind matters of war and peace, diplomats and soldiers, summit conferences and grandiloquent speeches. No doubt, it is in these glamorous spheres that the emotions of one nation toward another are shaped and where well-known history occurs.

The international relations of neighbors, however, have a far less noticeable and far less glamorous aspect. Their day-to-day relations are governed largely out of the public limelight. The inevitable problems of trade—the problems of the shared fisheries, the regulation of the boundary, the administration of continental defense—all these cannot be resolved by a simple decision in Washington or Ottawa. They require a plethora of continental institutions—a bureaucracy of Canadian-American relations.

The bureaucracy has grown as needs demanded. Parts of it are unique; parts of it are inadequate; parts of it are over-burdened; parts of it seem to serve no useful purpose at all; and as with most bureaucracies some parts duplicate the work of others. It is subject to all the laws of bureaucracies, Parkinson's included.

Nonetheless, this bureaucracy is the hard core of day-to-day U.S.–Canadian relations. And it provides a valuable, if unspectacular formula for success in the affairs between the two countries.

Recently, one Canadian commentator was somewhat more harsh on the system:

The structure is not founded in any treaty or agreement clearly setting out problem areas to be dealt with, and governing the principles and procedures to be followed. It is a patchwork of committees which meet now and then about this and that; in secret, remote from the public, and accounting for itself only through communiques and press releases which are normally full of good will but empty of useful information for either the parliaments of the two countries or the public. The structure does not bring a sense of permanence, nor continuity, nor definition, nor public participation to the conduct of the joint affairs of the two North American democracies.[1]

Accepting all that, and most of it rings all too true, thoughtful men will ask themselves whether the strength of U.S.-Canadian relations is best served by publicity to all its details within a carefully ordered system of institutions with carefully prescribed functions and authority. We would be the last to argue for secrecy in normal government procedures. Public attention, however, has seldom made men more rational—and in the world of diplomacy, the glare of lights frequently makes agreement, even minor agreement, impossible for otherwise rational men.

Similarly, progress in the growth of comfortable international relations stems not from an organized, precise, and legal structure of institutions, but from the ease with which agreement can be reached. The institutions must be flexible; they must be malleable; they must facilitate change; they must not impose discipline. A bureaucracy can encourage progress or stifle it. The purpose of the U.S.-Canadian bureaucracy should not be to preserve the status quo but to accommodate reform.

None of the Canadian-American institutions is more instructive of the past or more permanent for the future than the International Joint Commission. It is unique as a symbol of the relations between the North American democracies. We will discuss it at length. But first let us review the other institutions of the continent—the component parts of the U.S.-Canadian international bureaucracy.

128

The International Boundary Commission was established in 1925. It inspects the entire boundary periodically, prepares and replaces deteriorating boundary markers, keeps the boundary vistas clean of forest growth. In the case of a boundary dispute, the Commission has the power to define the location of a questionable point on the boundary line. It represents significant progress in international affairs. In the nineteenth century, the U.S. and Britain experimented with the concept of boundary arbitration by a foreign monarch. In 1827, they submitted the boundary dispute between Maine and New Brunswick to the King of the Netherlands, whose suggestion for settlement was considered unsatisfactory both by the British, who nonetheless tentatively agreed to accept it, and by the State of Maine, which was more adamant. It may be a prerequisite to success that an arbitrated settlement be disliked by both sides, but the International Boundary Commission has not yet been faced with a dilemma to approach the size of that which was imposed on the Dutch King 140 years ago. The job today appears to be routine.

The United States and Canada are members of a multitude of international commissions dealing with fishery resources and marine mammals. They are both members of five multilateral commissions: the Northwest Atlantic Fisheries Commission; the Inter-American Tropical Tuna Commission; the International Fur Seal Commission; the International Whaling Commission; and the High Seas Fisheries of the Northern Pacific Ocean. In addition there exist three bilateral U.S.–Canadian fishery institutions; the Great Lakes Fishery Commission; the International Pacific Halibut Commission; and the International Pacific Salmon Commission.

To the landlubber this collection of agencies may seem just another example of how government spawns no less prolifically than fish. But these institutions are the product of cooperation in a field which historically has been vitally important to the economy of both nations and today remains a significant source of income for regions in both countries. The historical intensity of the U.S.–Canadian debate over fisheries might best be illus-

129

trated by the following wire sent by the Governor of the State of Washington to the Secretary of State, which resulted in the withdrawal of a U.S.–Canadian Salmon Fisheries Treaty that the President had put before the Senate:

> Our legislature by unanimous vote of both houses protested this treaty and we are a part of the United States and it appears that we ought to have some rights even when they conflict with the unjust demands of Great Britain . . . Our people are not all children whose playthings should be taken away and given to older people, neither are they citizens of a weakling nation to have their heritage taken from them and given to another power.[2]

The institutions of defense we have discussed earlier. The Joint Board of Defense was created in 1940 and made permanent in 1947. Organized in two equal national sections, each with its own civilian chairman, the Board has representatives from the armed services and the Departments of External Affairs and State. Its task today is essentially to mesh the requirements of defense with the political atmosphere in which defense questions must be considered. It provides a more flexible forum for discussion than NORAD, which is essentially an administrative operation. It has the power only to recommend, and only then if unanimity is achieved.

NORAD was founded in 1957 but is the outgrowth of a bilateral military-planning group formed at the time of the founding of NATO. It is important to understand that even in the case of a direct air attack, NORAD cannot act on its own authority but only under orders from the Joint Chiefs of Staff in Washington and the Joint Chiefs of Staff Commission in Ottawa.

The third international defense institution is the Cabinet Committee on Joint Defense. Created in 1958, its members are the U.S. secretaries of State, Defense, and Treasury and the Canadian ministers for External Affairs, National Defence, and

Finance. The group meets infrequently to review defense relationships and to emphasize the political and economic aspects of today's international military problems. It cannot be considered a permanent part of the international U.S.–Canadian bureaucracy—but it should be viewed as an available and appropriate forum for the quiet but high-level discussions frequently required by sudden international crises.

The Joint Committee on Trade and Economic Affairs is a similar institution. It was established in 1953, has met only infrequently since then, and its role has not been well defined by active utilization. The United States members include the Secretaries of State, Treasury, Agriculture, Commerce, and Interior. The Canadian members are the Secretary of State for External Affairs and the Ministers of Finance, Trade and Commerce, Industry, and either Agriculture or Fisheries. They meet as administrators capable only of making commitments to the extent that they control their own departments. The Committee can be credited with laying the groundwork for the U.S.–Canadian automotive-parts agreement and for instigating the study of Messrs. Merchant and Heeney of principles to guide U.S.–Canadian relations.

Both the Merchant-Heeney Report and the Tupper Report recommended that the Joint Committee on Trade and Economic Affairs "establish a Joint Committee of Deputies to meet frequently on behalf of their principals and be available at short notice to consider any emerging problem." [3] As a standing or relatively permanent body, the Committee is not an efficient means for considering jointly the many areas of trade relations in which the two nations come into conflict. Joint consideration of policy does not mean occasional conscience-stricken attempts to salve the feelings of others—it means full, and reasonably constant, consultation on the details of policy between representatives of the two governments. The effectiveness of the Committee would be improved with more frequent meetings. The need for continuity is so great and the Committee membership so subject to change that

131

there is an urgent need for permanent deputies in continual contact.

Aside from the IJC, the last of the significant U.S.–Canadian institutions is the Canada–United States Interparliamentary Group. Established in 1959, the Group holds one meeting a year in each country, with twenty-four members of Parliament and twenty-four members of Congress attending. One of the authors has been a member of the United States delegation to many of these meetings. In fact, the Interparliamentary Group was established largely at the initiative of the Honorable Frank Coffin, who preceded the author to the Congress as a representative from the State of Maine.

Unfortunately the meetings of the Interparliamentary Group are more social than productive. Surely the purpose of the Group is not merely to have a good time but to help in the serious consideration of problems which beset the relations between the North American democracies.

We do not wish to imply that the meetings of the Canada–U.S. Interparliamentary Group have been without benefit to the two nations. Men such as the late Mark Drouin, a former Speaker of the Canadian Senate, and former Speaker of the House of Commons Alan McNaughton, Senator George Aiken and Congressman Cornelius Gallagher, Co-Chairmen of the U.S. delegation, have made many friends for their respective countries.

But the value of exchange of information is small compared to the constructive contribution which the Interparliamentary Group could make if it took unto itself a greater responsibility for action.

If each session were to identify one or two of the most pressing problems affecting Canadian–U.S. relations and were to create specific committees among its members to study these problems in some detail in the intervening time before the next parliamentary meeting, the Group would be able to make more constructive contributions to the settlement of issues.

We do not suggest greater publicity or greater formality for the meetings. We do suggest a more determined effort by the parliamentarians themselves to see their Group as a vehicle for initiative. They do not meet and should not meet as diplomatic representatives of their countries. They meet, and should meet, as legislators interested in common problems, and with the capacity to return to their respective capitals with specific recommendations for their governments.

On the American side, it is imperative that appointment to the Interparliamentary Group not be merely a prize awarded for party regularity—or for its potential political value to a politician in a state with numerous people of Canadian descent. The participants should have a real interest in U.S.–Canadian affairs. They should be briefed periodically on U.S.–Canadian relations by the State Department and their respective Congressional committees—not just in advance of parliamentary meetings, but on a continuing basis. They should recognize that because they do not represent the administration in Washington, they are free to innovate and initiate policy proposals that can shape the future of continental relations.

On the Canadian side, perhaps it would be valuable for the parliamentary representatives to be sufficiently detached from the leadership of the majority party that they neither are nor feel like formal representatives of the government. They should be chosen, in part, for their capacity to speak with a free mind and to return from the Interparliamentary Group sessions free to initiate changes in policy if they are called for.

In short, the Interparliamentary Group should be made a working body, with standing committees charged with the responsibility of proposing to the Group and to the two governments alternative courses of action to existing policy or innovations in existing relations.

If Canadian-American relations are to work; if the two continental democracies can build in North America a model for relations between independent nations, it will be the politicians who make it so. It is, after all, their job, more than any other, to shape the course which their nations will follow in the years ahead. This is why the Interparliamentary Group should take on a far greater responsibility than it has thus far.

This is why we also believe that smaller and more regional interparliamentary groups for members of the state and provincial legislatures could be beneficial for the future. Frequently the instances of dispute and the areas of opportunity in relations between the two countries arise in matters which constitutionally come under the jurisdiction of the states in the United States and the provinces in Canada. More active contact between the legislators of these neighboring political subdivisions would greatly facilitate the solution of difficult technical problems, the anticipation of issues of potential conflict, the development of mutual programs for the common benefit of the regions, and the growth of closer and more productive ties between the peoples of the two nations. Of course, it would be important for the Department of State to extend participating members of the state legislatures periodic briefings on U.S.–Canadian affairs and on the specific issues that may arise in the conduct of the joint sessions. But more important, the meetings should be kept informal and flexible so that progress is not impeded either by the dictates of conventional diplomacy or by an institutional structure that would substitute propriety for joint exploration.

Last, but greatest, among the institutions of the U.S.–Canadian bureaucracy is the International Joint Commission (IJC). No organization or institution has been more of a bulwark in the maintenance of strong and productive U.S.–Canadian relations. It was the IJC that accomplished most of the technical tasks leading to the great international cooperation in the St. Lawrence Seaway and the development of the Columbia River Basin. Among its many technical studies today are the vital issues of water pollution in the Great Lakes and the St. Lawrence River System and the fluctuating water levels of the Great Lakes.

It was appropriate that the 1909 treaty which founded the

Commission was signed by two of the world's greatest legal minds—James Bryce for Great Britain and Elihu Root for the United States. The concept of the Commission was and is an extraordinary example of what constructive international relations can mean—the solution of international problems, not by negotiation, but by an authoritative international body. The Commission is made up of American and Canadian sections, but when they sit together they take on an international personality. The members are not representatives of their governments but of a permanent tribunal for the solution of international controversies.

The functions of the IJC are both judicial and investigative. In some cases it can resolve disputes, in others it can merely explore disputes and recommend action. Before 1944, the IJC considered 50 cases, 39 of which were applications for the approval of specific projects and only 11 were requests from the governments for investigation. Since that date, however, 20 of the 32 cases before the IJC have been governmental referrals for investigation.[4]

Perhaps the greatest value of the IJC is not in its judicial decisions or in its technical studies. It is merely in its existence.

> . . . the true measure of the Commission's usefulness to the people of the United States and Canada lies not even so much in its positive as in its negative qualities, not so much in the cases it has actually settled as in the infinitely larger number of cases that never come before it for consideration, simply because the Commission is there, as a sort of international safety-valve, and therefore the sting is taken out of the situation.[5]

From this glowing description, one might assume that the Commission's purview was extremely broad. It is not. A creature of the Boundary Waters Treaty of 1909, the IJC is essentially designed as a vehicle to facilitate the coordinated and cooperative use of the boundary waters of the two countries. By the Treaty, IJC approval must be secured for any diversion or obstruction of boundary waters on either side of the border which would affect the natural level or flow of waters on the other side of the border and for any dams or obstructions below the boundary in rivers crossing the boundary or flowing out of boundary waters which would raise or lower the natural level of waters in the other country. And, in addition, any other matters relating to problems along the common frontier may be referred to the Commission for its study and recommendations. In many instances, the Commission, having made its recommendations, will continue to oversee their implementation by the governments involved.

The Commission is currently looking at the possibility of a waterway between the St. Lawrence and Hudson rivers through Lake Champlain; the cooperative development of the water resources of the Pembina River; regulation of the water levels of the Great Lakes; and pollution of the waters of the Red River, Lake Erie, Lake Ontario, and the international section of the St. Lawrence Seaway.

Other than its technical solutions, what real contribution to Canadian–U.S. relations does the IJC make? First of all, in its authority to approve or deny any action taken to divert or affect the boundary waters, the IJC has been a unique international tribunal. Nowhere else in the world have the people of two countries had the opportunity of appearing personally before an international institution with the authority of final judgment. In this sense alone, it is a history-making body.

But even more important, the IJC, as a permanent body, has developed a certain *esprit de corps* vital to the maintenance of constructive U.S.–Canadian relations on many technical matters which the two countries must resolve:

> A unique feature of this Commission, and one which differentiates it from similar organizations in the past, is that there is no casting vote . . . There is no umpire, drawn from outside and lacking intimate knowledge of the problems, whom each side would try to influence to its point of view. These six Commissioners, half American and half

Canadian, are pledged to a view-point that is American in the continental sense. They must regard the people on both sides of the boundary as equally entitled to their best possible judgment. There can be no "smartness" nor jockeying in such an organization. All six Commissioners represent the same broad international constituency . . .[6]

A review of world crisis spots today points to any number of international disputes over boundary waters. Israel and Jordan threaten to ignite the glowing embers of the Middle East passions over diversion of the waters of the River Jordan. Egypt and the Sudan seem locked in an interminable debate over rights to waters of the Nile River. And one phase of the India-Pakistan dispute is over the Indus River. In none of these crises are the protagonists blessed with the availability of an IJC, with an authoritative international tribunal with an independent reputation to provide the channels for peaceful resolution of the conflict.

It is our contention that just as the Commission has greatly served the interests of the two nations in the past, its functions and powers should be significantly expanded so as to serve the two nations over the "second hundred years."

Hesitancy is always appropriate in tinkering with proven international institutions. We should not lightly consider changing the International Joint Commission through renegotiation of the Canadian-American Boundary Waters Treaty of 1909. But of the U.S.–Canadian institutions, the IJC has above all served its purpose with excellence, and because of its past we believe that it may be the institution that can bring new excellence to the relations between the two countries—in a broad spectrum of areas with which it is not presently authorized to deal.

The Merchant-Heeney Report recommended that the Canadian and American governments examine jointly the wisdom and feasibility "of some extension of the Commission's functions." Ambassador Heeney has separately made the same point many times.

How should the IJC be expanded? First, it should be specifically empowered to consider and make recommendations relating to the continental development of water and energy resources.

In the previous chapter, we cited the potential benefits to both nations from a continental program of water-sharing and the preliminary step that both governments must take before such a program could ever come into being—including an exhaustive Canadian survey of water resources and water needs to assure that Canada would not merely be giving away resources that she would need in the years to come. If and when the two nations reach mutual agreement on the desirability of exploring continental plans for the sharing of water, hydroelectric power, and peaceful nuclear energy, it will be important for them to have in existence an international body authorized to make the extremely technical studies necessary to lay the basis for a constructive international agreement. The IJC today cannot undertake such a plan. It should be authorized to do so under the renegotiation of the Treaty by which it was established to provide it a more flexible charter. The IJC should be permitted to accept the charge of the two governments in any area calling for technical studies and recommendations.

Second, the definition of "boundary waters" under the 1909 Treaty should be extended to include the waters of Lake Michigan. In the preliminary article to the Boundary Waters Treaty, boundary waters are defined as "the waters from main shore to main shore of the lakes and rivers and connecting waterways, or the portions thereof, along which the international boundary passes, including all bays, arms and inlets thereof, but not including tributary waters which in their natural channels would flow into such lakes, rivers, and waterways or waters flowing from such lakes, rivers, and waterways, or the waters of rivers flowing across the boundary." By this definition, the waters of Lake Michigan are not included under the jurisdiction of the International Joint Commission. Article

138

3 of the Boundary Waters Treaty, in effect, declares that the IJC has no authority to consider matters relating to the diversion of waters which are not defined as "boundary waters."

Lake Michigan, however, is one of the Great Lakes and the other four Great Lakes come under IJC auspices. Diversion of waters from Lake Michigan lowers the water levels of all the lakes, thus affecting the boundary waters and Canadian as well as U.S. interests.

The city of Chicago has long had a program of waste disposal and uses the waters of Lake Michigan to flush its sewage down the Mississippi River into the Gulf of Mexico. Chicago's need should not be minimized, but such a program has a direct bearing on the economic interests of the Canadian people. A major water-diversion program of this kind is inappropriate without international cooperation and agreement.

It is ridiculous to persist in the illusion that the water levels of Lake Michigan are less important to the Canadians than the water levels of the other four Great Lakes. The Great Lakes are in effect one whole; what happens to one affects them all. It is equally ridiculous to argue, as some have argued, that Lake Michigan already comes within the treaty definition of boundary waters as a bay of Lake Huron. Lake Michigan does not come under the purview of the IJC. It should. And the Treaty should be renegotiated to include it.

The extension of the boundary-waters definition to include the waters of Lake Michigan would not be an extraordinary or unprecedented step, in view of the fact that Article 1 of the 1909 Treaty specifically states that the waters of Lake Michigan for the purposes of navigation will be considered as boundary waters under the treaty.

Third, we believe that the International Joint Commission should be a sufficiently broad and flexible institution to permit the two governments to refer to it technical problems of foreign-policy consideration.

There are a variety of different areas in which one government has taken the lead in a technical foreign-policy matter

139

and where cooperative technical discussions within an international forum might lead to a cooperative policy. For example, should the United States wish to follow the lead of the Canadian Government in the establishment of earmarked national forces on stand-by for potential call by the United Nations in peacekeeping operations, international discussions by technical experts under the International Joint Commission could benefit the United States Government immeasurably by providing it with the Canadian experience in this area.

Presumably, if the Government of Canada wished to follow the United States lead in placing one or more of its peaceful nuclear reactors under the safeguard and inspection system of the International Atomic Energy Agency, technical discussions with American experts under the aegis of the International Joint Commission could provide the Canadian Government the benefit of the experience gained in the United States.

But quite aside from technical and scientific matters, the IJC could play an expanding role in foreign-policy discussions between the two governments at the administrative level. It may be possible to explore, in secret, but away from the imposed formality of diplomacy, the avenues for Canadian initiative in foreign policy which would be beneficial to the interests of the United States, and vice versa. The expanded IJC would have no authority to act as an independent body in these areas, but it could make recommendations on the basis of joint studies, and it could be the source of considerable creativity in either united or compatible foreign policy.

The higher echelons of the International Joint Commission could be utilized by the two governments as a standing group to discuss in private the many disagreements the two nations may have in a broad spectrum of foreign-policy questions. We do not suggest that the International Joint Commission should be reconstituted to be the one and only locus of discussion on foreign-policy problems between the two governments. Quite the contrary, we propose merely that the IJC become one more of many channels of communication that can be utilized in the joint consideration of foreign-policy differences—and that it can be a particularly appropriate institution through which the two governments can share their technical expertise in some of the more intricate and scientific aspects of contemporary foreign policy.

A joint foreign policy is not essential—and in many cases it is not desirable. But joint consideration of foreign-policy problems is essential. And it is important to have an independent institution, capable of thought not dictated from Ottawa or Washington that can lead to responsible recommendations to the two governments for policy courses to be followed.

Fourth, and perhaps most important, we believe that the International Joint Commission should have the authority as an independent body to undertake studies and make recommendations without relying on the two governments to refer matters for its consideration. It should, in short, have the power to initiate its own studies—the power to prod and needle the two governments, the power of conscience—the power to explore the future and to challenge the two governments to shape that future in the most constructive way. All this simply means that the IJC should be given the right to think on its own as an independent agency charged with a highest priority of concern for the development of a model for relations between independent nations on the North American continent.

The idea is not new. As long ago as 1932, it was proposed that "the Commission should have an adequate power of initiative in all these matters rather than be forced to depend on the two governments every time a contingency arises."[7] The Commission we advocate is a Commission with an authority to anticipate the future—its opportunities and its dangers. Too often the United States concerns itself with North American problems only when Canada confronts it with a direct challenge or when the crisis is obvious, and obviously upon us. An independent joint Commission, staffed by competent and respected appointees from the two countries, could do much to overcome the American tendency to be preoccupied with problems in more distant parts of the globe.

The IJC has not simply proven its merit as a technical commission charged with technical tasks. It has proven its capacity to provide continental leadership—sometimes to governments that are reluctant to act or do not see the challenge clearly. This can be the institution for the future. And from it may come the forms which will allow the North American democracies to build a new model of international relations where mutual respect for independence and mutual attention to the future—to its opportunities and its obligations—will enable our continent more fully to serve the interests of all men and all nations. A bureaucracy seldom is thought capable of creativity. But the bureaucracy of U.S.–Canadian relations can be an exception if we have the courage to build the future upon its extraordinary past.

Chapter IX

Mobility: The Symbol of Progress

For the historians a century from now, it may seem a startling fact that in this age of easy mobility, and despite the almost total absence of legal restrictions on international movement between the two countries, immigration and emigration between the United States and Canada are far smaller today than they were when to move was a far more arduous task.

Emigration may expand rapidly again. If history is any judge, it will do so only when the opportunities in one country seem extraordinarily greater than they are in the other.

> It has always been and is still true that whenever the opportunity glows more brightly on one side of the boundary than on the other the movement expands in rapid response and citizens of one country move to the other with almost the same easy disregard of political boundaries that characterized their fathers before them.[1]

The immigration with which Americans are most familiar is the movement of people from Europe to the United States in search not only of economic opportunity but of political freedom too. That motive has been largely absent from the flow of emigrants across the U.S.–Canadian border. There were, of course, the loyalists who left the United States at the time of the Revolution and emigrated to Canada in order to escape the vengeance of the rebels. And shortly before the United States Civil War, many American Negroes found their way to Canada through the underground railroad in search of a haven from slavery. And no doubt many French Canadians throughout history have sought in the United States a greater tolerance of their culture than they felt existed in Canada.

But the dominant theme of emigration between Canada and the United States has been economic opportunity. Until recent times, the ebb and flow of movement from one country to the other was part and parcel of the westward expansion and the opening of the new frontiers of the New World.

From the American Revolution until the War of 1812, there was a fairly constant flow of Americans into British North America. On the eve of the Revolution, it was estimated that eight out of every ten persons of Upper Canada in Quebec were of American descent. The War of 1812 stopped this flow both by diverting the expansion westward rather than northward and by creating, even at this early date, anti-American sentiment in Canada.

From the Civil War to the turn of the century, as the American West developed rapidly so too did Canadian emigration to the United States—both to the farmlands of the Middle West and to the new industrial centers of New England. On the other hand, with the opening of the Canadian West at the turn of the century the emigration flowed the other way, with hundreds of thousands of Americans, mostly farmers, seeking opportunities in the pioneer lands of western Canada. Between 1901 and 1911, the number of American-born persons in Canada increased by 137 per cent. This flow of Americans was augmented by an almost equal number of returning Canadians who had earlier left their country for the American Middle West and now came home to their own land. This prewar period also saw the beginning of the establishment of United States branch plants in Canada, with increasing numbers of Americans following American capital into Canada.

Post–World War I brought a fantastic industrial boom in the United States and such a great influx of immigrants from Canada and around the world that in 1924 the United States began to apply rigid immigration quotas. Nonetheless, the

1920's saw a great influx of Canadians into the United States. When the crash came in 1929, immigration in both countries came to a screeching halt—with a heavy inclination of emigrants to return to their native countries. The trend continued until World War II. The 1940 U.S. Census shows that the number of Canadian-born in the United States had decreased almost 250,000 over the ten-year period.

Both countries have experienced relatively full employment since the end of World War II. The two have provided similar economic opportunities. A constant two-way flow of Canadians and Americans crossing the border has resulted.

Today Canadian emigrants outnumber American emigrants three to one. Nonetheless the impact is felt far more severely in Canada than in the United States. Despite the larger Canadian emigration, the percentage of U.S. emigrants in the Canadian population is far larger than the percentage of Canadian emigrants in the American population. Similarly, the Canadian emigration has taken the form of men seeking employment—frequently professionally trained men; while American emigration has often represented men seeking investment opportunities for their capital, resulting in an immense impact on the Canadian economy.

In the recent past, approximately 15,000 Americans a year moved to Canada, and until 1966 somewhere between 30,000 and 40,000 Canadians a year moved to the United States. These figures are small compared to the century highpoints of 120,000 U.S. emigrants to Canada in 1913 and 101,000 Canadian emigrants to the U.S. in 1925. In view of today's ease of mobility and the substantial growth in the over-all population of the two countries, current immigration figures compared with those earlier in the century are testimony to the extraordinary economic prosperity and opportunities in both countries today.

Who are the U.S emigrants to Canada, what do they do, and where do they live? U.S. emigration to Canada in 1965 was the highest since the end of World War II. Exactly 15,-

145

143 Americans moved to Canada in 1965—an increase of 21 per cent over 1964 and 35 per cent over 1960. Of total Canadian immigration in 1965 (147,000) the United States group was the third largest—after Great Britain and Italy.

According to the Canadian Government Immigration Service, most of the U.S. emigrants, as might be predicted, come from states along the border, with over 2,300 from New York alone in 1965.

The largest group of Americans in Canada are employed as farmers—a result of heavy U.S. emigration to the Canadian plains in the first part of this century. In more recent years, the U.S. movement to Canada has consisted of highly skilled laborers, scientific personnel, and professional men. Over half the emigrants to Canada in the last two decades have practiced a profession or worked at a skilled trade.[2] Of the 15,000 U.S. emigrants to Canada in 1965, 204 were "entrepreneurs" planning to invest in Canadian business or open new enterprises; 683 were persons in the managerial class; 2,694 were persons with professional or technical training; and 2,578 others had other specific skills.[3] (Obviously, no statistics on the number of U.S. young men trying to avoid the draft are available.)

When Americans emigrate to Canada, they distribute themselves equally over the country. They do not, as is common with many immigrant groups, live in isolated communities or in bloc centers. They do mingle with the Canadian population on a fairly free basis, which is one reason for the widespread Canadian knowledge of U.S. history, culture, and politics.

Of the 1965 U.S. emigrants to Canada more than 6,000 gave Ontario as their planned destination; 3,400 planned to settle in British Columbia; 2,200 in Quebec; and 1,600 in Alberta.[4]

In the search for a Canadian national identity, it is important to realize that intermingling of immigrant groups in Canada has not followed the melting-pot ways that have been described broadly as at least one basis for the national identity of the United States. In recent years, sociologists have been

146

debunking the automatic assumption made by political scientists for generations that the United States is in fact a true melting pot—where foreign nationalities are subsumed in one large happy family. In fact, most northern industrial cities in the United States contain highly organized ethnic communities, which, even after many generations, have not really begun to blend together. But American nationalism preceded these groups, and each of them shares a form of American allegiance without necessarily recognizing the full validity of the claims of others to an equal share in their new country.

In Canada, a sense of national identity did not precede the arrival of substantial immigrant groups. They have made the search for national identity far more difficult. Ethnic barriers exist in both countries. The remnants of national pride among immigrant groups exist in both countries. But there is a commanding, if ill-defined, nationalism in the United States that does not exist in Canada. It is a source of strength in the United States; its absence is a source of weakness in Canada.

With a similar culture and identical language, Americans in Canada, just as English-Canadians in the United States, are not subject to this kind of bloc treatment—although there is a certain suspicion of American businessmen in Canada stemming from fear of American domination of the Canadian economy.

One further statistic is important to measure the significance of movement across the border. There has been a much higher rate of naturalization of Americans in Canada than Canadians in the U.S. In 1941, fully 75 per cent of the American-born population in Canada had been naturalized. That figure is not as high today, indicating that many Americans now move to Canada to follow business investments but not necessarily to establish permanent residence. The rate of U.S. naturalization of immigrants from Canada is relatively low, indicating that they too are seeking temporary employment opportunities and expect to return home.

Who are the Canadian emigrants to the United States, what

147

do they do, and where do they live? Because their patterns of life in the United States are far different, it is essential to distinguish between English-Canadians and French-Canadians. Since 1820, almost 3.5 million Canadians have moved to the United States, a figure larger than the total U.S. immigration from England. Of these, roughly 70 to 75 per cent have been English-Canadian.

One major reason for Canadian emigration to the United States is completely different from any American reason for emigration to Canada.

> What attracts them is not only cheaper goods, higher pay, more challenging opportunities, but the simple matter of climate. No analysis can get far from the fact that most of it is cold and a bit dreary—with five-month winters the rule, average January lows below zero in the Provinces, 80 inches of snow a winter in Ottawa, an average of 5 hours a day of sunshine in Montreal. Thus, sunny California is the No. 1 destination of immigrating Canadians. Last year [1964] 10,738 headed southward to make it their home.[5]

Also the geographic north-south "pull" is far stronger than the east-west ties within Canada; the "pull" attracts Canadians to their sister states across the border. Canadians in the United States tend to settle in fairly specific areas: in New England, New York, the North Central States, and most recently on the Pacific Coast. Nearly 80 per cent of all Canadians in the United States live in the border states plus Massachusetts, Connecticut, Rhode Island, California, and Oregon. Detroit, New York City, Boston, and Los Angeles have larger Canadian populations than most Canadian cities.

In the nineteenth century, the Canadian influx into the United States was largely agricultural. In more recent years, the trend has been toward professional people seeking high-paying jobs.

Throughout the twentieth century, there have been two other major areas of Canadian contribution to the American population make-up. First, because the United States has become the film capital of the world, talented Canadians in the fields of entertainment have sought the American stage. The list seems almost endless: Mary Pickford, Beatrice Lillie, Raymond Massey, Walter Pidgeon, Walter Houston, Norma Shearer—simply to mention a few. The second field is even more vital to the United States. Many Canadian scholars have sought positions in the American academic community. Even a brief list reflects both on the advanced-education system in the United States and on the relatively slow growth of Canadian higher education: John Kenneth Galbraith, noted professor of economics at Harvard University; Herbert Dougall, professor of finance at Stanford University; Nathan Keyfitz, professor of sociology at the University of Chicago; John Logan, president of Rose Polytechnical Institute in Terre Haute, Indiana; John L. McKelvey, professor of obstetrics and gynecology at the University of Minnesota; Robert Poleson, professor of sociology at Cornell; Carl A. Roebuck, professor of classics at Northwestern University. This is one more example of the "brain drain" which concerns many Canadian educators as they contemplate the development of their own scientific industries and their own institutions of higher education.

Like Americans in Canada, English-Canadians in the United States almost fully assimilate into their communities. Because their cultural, religious, political, and language backgrounds are so similar, their integration into the American communities is almost completely unencumbered. The English-Canadian immigrant

. . . comes into a community which speaks his tongue and in which he immediately feels at home. He sends his children, not to parish schools, but to the public schools, and he reads not the Canadian but the American press. He still has a sentimental devotion to the land of his birth, but culturally he becomes one in spirit with the American.[6]

149

The English-Canadian finds no real reason to live in blocs. He is separated from the community but is part of it. Nonetheless he does tend to view his residence in the United States as temporary, and therefore his rate of U.S. naturalization is not as high as it is among most European immigrants who have made a permanent break with their native home.

The French-Canadian immigrants in the United States have written quite a different story. From 25 to 30 per cent of the Canadians in the United States are French-Canadian. By and large they have not brought the same advanced skills to the United States. They live in very specific parts of the country. And they have not been as easily assimilated as their English-Canadian brethren.

There have been two major influxes of French-Canadians into the United States—each with a distinct history. The first was the trip of the Acadians from Canada to the Louisiana Gulf in 1775, undertaken to avoid the new British rule. In many cases these farmers sought refuge in the French Catholic community around New Orleans. They shunned the urban New Orleans life and for almost two hundred years have remained a rural, close-knit people in the Louisiana coastal marsh.

Today more than 250,000 French-speaking people occupy Acadiana and participate in the same occupations as their ancestors—they hunt and sell fur; they farm rice and sugar; they tend cattle. And today they participate in the search for oil and sulphur off the Louisiana coast. They are an ingrown community—so much so that any further emigration to them from Canada today is very minimal and might be personally very difficult.[7]

Except for the Acadians, the major French-Canadian migration to the United States took place between 1850 and 1930 and centered on the mill and river towns of New England. The Civil War provided an influx of French-Canadians recruited by the textile mills to replace men serving in the Northern Army in the Civil War. But the greatest movement

150

came in the period of extraordinary prosperity in the United States between 1900 and 1928. Since the Depression, French-Canadian migration out of Canada and into New England has been small.

Today there are more than 1 million French-Canadians in New England as a whole, and more than 400,000 French-Canadians in Massachusetts alone—these figures include fourth and fifth generations.

The French-Canadian immigrants were considered "semi-skilled" workers in 1910 and for the most part still are today. They worked in the New England mills, and as these have disappeared, they have weathered periods of unemployment until the growth of small industries could provide jobs.

Unlike the English-Canadians, the French-Canadians have remained a national bloc. Their immigration patterns have been more similar to those established by European nationalities. The first German settlers in the United States moved to the central states, and the large concentration of German ethnic background is today in Iowa and Wisconsin and Illinois, where new German immigrants have come to join the pioneers that preceded them. Similarly, new Hungarian and Polish immigrants, arriving in New York and Boston, followed the routes of those who came before and joined them in Cleveland and Detroit and Buffalo. So too with the French-Canadians. There are today large concentrations of French-Canadians throughout New England—in cities like Biddeford, Maine (almost 100 per cent French-Canadian); Manchester, New Hampshire (almost 90 per cent French-Canadian); Woonsocket, Rhode Island; Lewiston, Maine; Lowell, Massachusetts; Fall River, Massachusetts; New Bedford, Massachusetts; Worcester, Massachusetts; Nashua, New Hampshire; and Central Falls, Rhode Island.

The French-Canadian community in New England is not an isolated community. It is an insulated community. It participates in civic affairs—and frequently controls them. But the language, the religion, the education, and the culture are

French-Canadian. Only now in the fifth and sixth generation, is intermarriage with non-French-Canadians common. There are 179 French-Canadian parishes in New England which speak nothing but French; 107 others where French-Canadians are in the majority and the pastor speaks French; and still 142 more where French-Canadians number over 50 per cent of the congregation.

They have had their own daily and weekly newspapers published in French. At one time there were 30 Franco-American newspapers in New England, including dailies and weeklies.

The Catholic parishes frequently operate their own schools which teach in French. French-Canadian children generally go to parochial French-Canadian high schools. It is still true that in any home where the parents are over thirty-five years old, French is the language of the house. And finally, unlike any other national group in the United States, their native homes—in Quebec—are still close enough to visit frequently in order to rekindle whatever national feelings their life in the United States might have tended to modify:

> . . . the Association Canado Americaine, with head-quarters in Manchester, has one-third of its members in the Province of Quebec. All groups meet in general conventions and carry on an interchange of visits. French Canadian newspapers and books are read by Franco-Americans. Lecturers from French Canada are invited to the United States. Relatives visit one another. Many Franco-American parents send their children, boys and girls, to the colleges and convents of Quebec. In substance, relations are of a cultural nature, economical, political, and social ties being negligible.[8]

In the United States this kind of ethnic-bloc living is standard practice. It is accepted without significant incident, perhaps because no single group is so large as to control completely any segment of the American economic or political scene. French Canada poses a greater problem to the Canadian nation than any individual ethnic group does to the United States. As a result, it is possible that if the gulf between the English- and French-Canadians continues to grow, a new wave of French-Canadian immigration could take place to enlarge the French-Canadian population of New England.

Canada historically has been and is today an immigrant-seeking country. The four purposes of its immigration policy since World War II have been described essentially as: first, to increase the population of Canada; second, to facilitate the admittance of new immigrants likely to become good citizens; third, to plan the immigration movement so that it does not make any fundamental alteration in the character of the Canadian nation; and fourth, to regulate the number of newcomers to the capacity of the Canadian economy to absorb them.[9] Canada is looking for skilled people to man its new industries and universities. It is apparent that its economic growth will attract newcomers from Europe and the United States—and they in turn will contribute to a continued economic growth. The dominant fact of Canadian immigration policy is a simple one: "The fact remains that our country must continue to expand even beyond its considerable development of the past years. It needs more than 19,000,000 people to populate its vast domain of 3,500,000 square miles." [10]

If Canada has an immigration problem, it is not in its capacity to attract skilled people from abroad. It is the incapacity to retain the skilled people in its own population, who have over a period of years been tempted to seek economic prosperity and opportunity in United States businesses and academic institutions. Almost 75 per cent of Canadian immigration to the United States is in the professional or skilled-labor groups. One analysis in the 1950's showed that in the years 1951–55, Canada saw nearly twice as many of its professionally qualified people emigrate to the United States as it saw professional people from the United States come to Canada. In addition, in the five-year period, 66,000 graduates from Canadian universities left for the United States.[11]

Although it is probably true that many of the professionally

153

qualified people leaving Canada do so only with the expectation of temporary employment in the United States and have every intention to return to Canada, the "brain drain" is a serious problem for the Canadians to face. It will become more serious if the trend is fed by a sudden explosion in the U.S. application of modern technology, which seems likely.

Even more serious than the "brain drain" of engineers and scientific people for American business and business research is the drain of Canadian academic talent to the constantly expanding institutions of higher education in the United States. Nothing is more vital to the Canadian future than the development of its own institutions of higher learning. And nothing is more vital to that development than the availability of qualified faculty talent. It is estimated that every day an average of four physicians, engineers, scientists, or university teachers leave Canada for the United States.[12] The problem for the future of the Canadian economy is a severe one.

Unintentionally, the United States has contributed to its severity. In 1965, the Congress passed and the administration signed into law a new immigration policy. It was a welcome step because it completely eliminated the obnoxious national-quota system of immigration. It replaced the old, irrational, and discriminatory law with a system based on two fundamental principles, each of which may have a serious impact on Canadian emigration.

The first principle of the new immigration law is that admittance into the United States will be closely related to the skills which the immigrant might bring with him. Describing the impact of the new law, the Director of the United States Immigration Services in Ottawa said that there would be three lists for emigrants preparing to move to the United States.[13] The first would be for those who qualified to work in the United States "automatically"—doctors, scientists, engineers, or those who can fill U.S. shortages.

The second and largest list would be for people with a specific employer in the United States to go to, an employer who would attest to authorities that there is no resident in the United States to fill the job. The third list would be for those who do not automatically qualify, such as those looking for menial jobs as service station attendants, for example, or for those jobs for which U.S. citizens could be easily trained.

Clearly, the operation of the new U.S. immigration law places a premium on the talent of those whom the Canadians fear losing the most. The new regulations have already had their impact on both the make-up and the quantity of Canadian emigration. The figure for fiscal 1966 was 10,000 below the 1965 figure—or a decline of 26 per cent.

The second basic thesis of the new U.S. immigration law is contained in two large hemispheric quotas, replacing the national-quota system. As the law now stands, beginning in mid-1968 there will be a total quota for all Western Hemisphere countries of immigration into the U.S. of 120,000. Furthermore, the law will be operated on a first-come-first-served basis in accordance with the guidelines listed above. This means that there is no assurance that immigration from Canada to the U.S. will remain unlimited. Total Western Hemisphere immigration to the United States in the fiscal year 1966 was 153,196. There is no reason to believe that this immigration will not grow rather than recede. At the time the immigration law was being debated in the U.S. Congress, Canadian Immigration Minister Jack Nicholson welcomed it: "We've been increasingly concerned with migration of Canadians to the United States and my Department had intended to take steps to reverse the flow." [14]

What may not have been fully understood is that while the hemispheric quota system may limit the Canadian emigration to the United States, it probably will have no effect on the "brain drain." If Canadian emigration is limited it will be the unskilled workers who will not get in.

We believe in the basic theory of free and unlimited immigration between contiguous countries. The new immigration law is a distinct improvement over the global system that it

155

replaced. It brings to this sphere of international relations a sense of morality which is compatible with the morality the United States seems always to preach. Its hemispheric quotas seem also to be a realistic application of the fact that the United States cannot absorb all who may wish to get in.

But for the sake of continental relations, we believe it would be appropriate if the United States opened its doors wide to its two contiguous neighbors, Canada and Mexico. There will be problems. In the Mexican case, domestic political considerations in the United States make unlikely the acceptance of the theory. In the Canadian case, the Canadian Government may wish to decline the offer in order to help reverse the flow of Canadian talent south of the border. If such a theory of free migration between contiguous countries were adopted it would have to be limited to the native-born population. It would be imperative to avoid the situation where citizens of third countries could emigrate to Canada merely as a way-station for their eventual emigration to the United States.

The basic problem of the "brain drain" from Canada cannot be resolved by a restrictive U.S. immigration policy without severely jeopardizing the progressive bases of U.S.–Canadian relations. The mobility across the U.S.–Canadian border and the unrestricted freedom to travel, visit, and live in the two countries has symbolized the unique relationship on the North American continent. As we look forward to the next century of continental cooperation—its opportunities and its obligations to provide a model for international relations between nations —this is no time to restrict that freedom of mobility.

The solution to the "brain drain" from Canada must come from other quarters. We have earlier suggested that U.S. businesses in Canada, under U.S. administration guidelines, might be encouraged to undertake their research operations in Canada rather than at their home plants in the United States, in order to employ significant Canadian engineers and scientists in their own country. But that will be only a partial answer.

156

The real answer can only be supplied by the Canadian Government: First, to encourage economic development and second, to encourage the growth of higher education, where Canadian academic talent can be employed and trained.

There must, as well, be a strengthening of the U.S. education system and an awareness of Canada, so that American talent can know of the opportunities for growth and personal achievement in the Canadian economy and academic community. Thus we return to a basic theme—the growth of a model for relations between independent nations on the North American continent depends upon a growing awareness by Americans of the history, culture, politics, and opportunities of Canada. American ignorance of Canada has been the greatest source of continental strain in the past. American awareness of Canada can be the greatest source of continental strength in the future.

Chapter X

An Appalling Ignorance

Every proposition has those who believe and those who doubt. And there are those in the United States who doubt that American ignorance of Canada is as widespread as we have suggested.

Students of U.S.–Canadian affairs know full well how little treatment Canadian problems and Canadian achievement receive in the American press. They know the lack of attention which Canadian government and history receive in American education. They know the truth in a recent editorial in *American Heritage:*

> If Americans have any view of Canada at all, it is generally that reflected . . . in the familiar Northland of the movies, where the Mountie (played by Nelson Eddy) always gets his man. It is a dream world where redcoats still parade, bootleggers replenish their stocks, and all the explorers are named for automobiles, and Evangeline never dries her tears. It is a good, stirring set of misconceptions . . .[1]

But any proposition should be tested, and we have done so. With the cooperation of high-school principals, teachers, and students in both countries we conducted a brief examination of high-school seniors to test their knowledge of the most basic facts about their neighboring country. The full results are printed in the Appendix.

The exam tested only "surface" knowledge—only the most

158

simple forms of awareness in one country of the happenings in the other. Such a test cannot prove in-depth knowledge or understanding of the affairs of another country. It can prove, however, the absence of in-depth knowledge of the affairs of another country—and in this case did so.

The test consisted of eleven questions about the neighboring country. Each U.S. question had its exact counterpart on the Canadian exam. The test was administered to 1,000 American and 1,000 Canadian high-school seniors. In the United States, it was given at twenty separate schools in twelve separate states along the Canadian border. In Canada, it was administered at eighteen separate high schools from Prince Edward Island to British Columbia.

All but 9 of the 1,000 Canadian high-school students could identify the capital of the United States. Only 329, or one-third of the 1,000 American high-school seniors knew that Ottawa was the Canadian capital; 230 thought it was Quebec; 178 guessed Montreal; 58 chose Toronto; and 36 Ontario. One brave soul said that Providence was the capital of Canada.

All but one Canadian student could identify Lyndon Johnson as the American President. Three hundred twenty-eight Americans identified Lester Pearson, no matter how his name was spelled (Patterson, McPearson, MacPherson, Ester Person, etc.). Harold Wilson was named by a number of Americans as were Harold Macmillan and Sir Alec Douglas-Home. Other interesting nominees included Averell Harriman, Charles de Gaulle, and Ludwig Erhard.

Six hundred ninety-four Canadian students (69.4 per cent) could identify President Johnson's political party. Surprisingly, 22 per cent of the Canadians identified the President as a Republican, which might prove equally distressing to both Republicans and Democrats. One student believed that President Johnson was a member of the Social Credit Party.

Only 13 per cent (133) of the American students could identify Prime Minister Pearson's party. A number more, but not many, confused the Liberal Party with the Labor Party. But

76.2 per cent of all the Canadian students were able to identify Barry Goldwater as the leader of the opposition party in the last United States elections. Credit was given for frequent distortions of the name, such as Harry Goldwater, Larry Goldwater, Arthur Goldwater, Goldboro, Goldsmith, Golding, Goldberg, and Stillwater. Credit was not given however for such nominees as Kennedy, Humphrey, Nixon, Scranton, Lodge, Nelson Rockefeller, John D. Rockerfellow, and John Diefenbaker.

The American students had a much harder time. Only 145 (14.5 per cent) could identify Diefenbaker as the leader of the opposition party in the last Canadian election. Again credit was given for distortions of the name such as: "Mr. Dusendorfer." Frequent confusion with British politicians appeared here too: from Macmillan to Wilson to Home and even to Cromwell. Ian Smith and Estes Kefauver received one vote apiece.

Fully 98.8 per cent of the Canadians could name two American states, and 68 per cent of the Americans could name two Canadian provinces. The Canadians tended to name states close to their own provinces, although Texas was more frequently named than any other single state. A number of Canadians tended to elevate American cities to statehood and one voted for Mexico as the fifty-first state. The Americans tended to be most familiar with the name of Quebec, but many seemed to remember the unusual name of Saskatchewan, although few could spell it. Here too, Providence received a vote as a province, as did London, Albuquerque, and Ecuador.

All the students were asked: "What is the name of the U.S.-Canadian defense organization?" A surprisingly small 25.5 per cent of the Canadians answered NORAD, although a good many more answered the DEW line. A pitifully small 7 per cent of American students named NORAD. Americans frequently made a valiant alphabetical stab with USCDO, working from the phraseology of the question. Typically, some Canadians reversed the formula and produced CUSDO. Other

160

answers included Conelrad, SEATO, UNESCO, Interpol, and the "blue line." Many Americans answered "the Royal Canadian Mounted Police." Our vote for the most ingenious answer goes to the American student who named "the Great Northern Lights."

Further, 85.6 per cent of all Canadians and 73.1 per cent of all Americans said that the neighboring country was a member of NATO. Since each student had a 50 per cent chance of being right, even with a guess, actual knowledge of NATO membership might be a little less in both countries.

Of the Canadians, 70.2 per cent said that the United States was a member of the Organization of American States. Only 46.1 per cent of the American students, however, said that Canada was not a member of the OAS. With a 50 per cent chance of being right, the American answers to this question were distressingly weak.

High-school students probably should not be expected to identify their nation's ambassadors in foreign capitals, and the test proved that they couldn't. Only 14 of the 1,000 Canadian students could name Ritchie as the Canadian Ambassador in Washington. This may in part be explained by the fact that Canada appointed a new ambassador only one month before the exam was taken. On the other hand, both the old ambassador and the ambassador-designate were named Ritchie. Others nominated for the post by Canadian students included Paul Martin, James Diefenbaker, Dean Rusk, Avril Haryman, Adlaide Stevenson, Emmit Cabbot Lodge, Bobby Hull, James Minifie, and even Stanley R. Tupper.

Not a single American student could identify J. Walton Butterworth as the United States Ambassador in Ottawa—although one Canadian student believed he was the Canadian Ambassador in Washington. Rusk, Lodge, Pearson, Stevenson, Diefenbaker, and Hull were named by the Americans also. There was a surprising tendency to say "there is none," or "there is no specific one."

Each group of students was asked to identify the official

161

language of the other country. Not surprisingly, 98.6 per cent of the Canadians identified English as the U.S. language. A number seemed intent on differentiating between types of English with such answers as: "Americanized English," "American —a type of English," "American (almost English)," and "English (corrupted)."

Only 10.5 per cent of the Americans correctly identified both English and French as official languages of Canada. The vast majority listed either English or French, and surprisingly French was listed more often than English. One American student was confident that the Canadians spoke Portuguese.

Finally the students were asked: "What is the population of the United States?" and "What is the population of Canada?" Of the Canadian students, 42.3 per cent placed the U.S. population somewhere between 150 million and 225 million. Only 13.5 per cent of the American students placed the Canadian population between 15 million and 25 million. The Canadian answers varied from 25 million to 60 billion to "white." The American answers ranged from 25,000 to 50 billion to "a lot," to "French." And in a tribute to the new math, one Canadian student correctly placed the U.S. population at "1.90×10^8."

Cumulatively, the Canadian students answered 69.7 per cent of all the questions correctly. The American score was 19.3 per cent. While the results of the exam should be distressing to Americans, they should not be the source of great joy in Canada. They are, in large measure, a reflection of the publicity process on the North American continent. In Canada, it is impossible not to know about the United States. In fact, some Canadian educators are concerned that Canadian students may know too much about the United States. As one Canadian student wrote at the bottom of his exam: "Could tell you less about Canada." Canadian national identity does not depend upon Canadian knowledge of the United States; it depends upon Canadian knowledge of Canada.

But progressive international relations upon the North American continent do depend upon American knowledge about Canada, and the American test scores attest undeniably to an

162

appalling ignorance of Canada in the United States. The only favorable light to be shed upon the results is in comparison with the results of a similar exam given thirty-four years earlier. At that time, only 21 per cent of the American students could name the Canadian capital, while today 33 per cent can. At that time, only 14 per cent could name the Canadian prime minister, while today 33 per cent can.[2]

Both tests, thirty-four years apart, reveal an inclination by American students to think of Canada in terms of Great Britain. Both showed a frequent tendency to confuse the British and Canadian prime ministers.

Whatever comfort might be gained from the feeling that American student knowledge of Canada is increasing might, however, be merely an illusion created by the decision to test only students in states bordering on Canada or the Great Lakes. In a survey of high-school seniors in Colorado, Connecticut, and Maryland, conducted recently, only 2 per cent could identify the Canadian prime minister.[3]

It can hardly be denied that "Canadian forbearance with American ignorance rather than American knowledge of Canadian customs has brought about the degree of harmony that does exist between the two countries."[4]

But Americans can hardly be complacent in the expectation that Canadian forbearance will be everlasting. The best we can expect, within present levels of understanding, is that the two nations will continue to get along at peace. The opportunity to create a model of international relations on the North American continent will be lost if the United States does not soon awake to the fact that its ignorance of Canada and its accompanying tendency to take Canada and Canadians for granted denies Canadian independence the respect it must have if progressive international relations between the two countries are to be built.

The problems of education on Canada in the United States are threefold: primary and secondary education; college and university education; public-affairs and adult education.

As the test results showed, any knowledge that students in

163

the United States gain about Canada in their elementary and secondary education is most likely incidental to other courses that they take. Only one high school of the twenty tested showed even the slightest evidence of serious effort at teaching the students about Canadian affairs. Obviously, the farther away from the Canadian border, the less likely it is that secondary or elementary schools would inject Canadian subjects into the curriculum.

Most American high-school students seem familiar with Canada only to the degree that they are familiar with the history of the War of 1812. And in most schools, even the War of 1812 is barely given any attention. We can only hope that local and state education leaders, in the growing realization that progressive U.S.–Canadian relations are threatened by U.S. failure to understand their importance, will seek to inject into the curriculum of U.S. high schools some appreciation of continental, not just American, history; continental, not just American, culture; continental, not just American, politics and government.

The broad network of local World Affairs Councils and foreign-policy discussion groups in American cities across the United States has created significant concern for world affairs and foreign-policy problems in the secondary-education programs of the public schools. As is so often the case, these programs have concentrated on crisis areas—on the strange, the exotic, the far distant, and the obviously critical. If equal attention were given to the significance of North American international relations, meaningful progress could be made in laying the foundation for a far greater awareness of Canada in the United States.

The federal and state governments in the United States could and should publicly encourage trips by high-school seniors to the seats of Canadian government in Ottawa and the provincial capitals. It is common practice for American high-school groups to spend their spring vacation or some other period during the academic year on a visit to Washington to study firsthand the operations of their government. Nothing could be more beneficial in the growth of any democracy. But it would be equally valuable, where feasible, for high schools in states along the Canadian border to plan for students' trips to visit and study Canadian Government institutions in Ottawa and the provincial capitals. This kind of program might leave an indelible impression of Canadian nationhood and institutions on the minds of American young people—and thereby help to make more permanent the American concern for Canadian interest.

At the college and university level, the problem is no less severe. A 1927 study showed only 19 American universities and colleges offering courses in Canadian history. A more recent study in 1958 showed only 38 U.S. collegiate institutions offering work in Canadian history. Twenty-four of the 38 were the product of postwar interest in foreign affairs.[5]

Few universities maintain significant library collections in Canadian history or literature. Prominent among them are Harvard, Wisconsin, Yale, Columbia, Michigan, Minnesota, and Rochester. Programs of Canadian studies at Duke, Michigan, Harvard, and Maine, while excellent, provide guidance only to a relatively small number of students and are the only broad Canadian studies programs in existence in American universities.

A handful of small colleges located in border states are offering Canadian studies of a limited nature. Ricker College of Houlton, Maine, comes to mind as one small college doing a very creditable job with such a program.

Student-exchange programs between the two countries at the collegiate or graduate level are distressingly small. Each year there are more Canadian students studying in the United States than there are from any other country. But the number still is less than 10,000, as compared to the 7,500 Indian students. Far more appalling, however: There are fewer than 3,000 American students who go to Canada each year for study at Canadian colleges and universities. Many of these are graduate students in medicine or in some special field where a particular

Canadian graduate program offers an outstanding course un-related to U.S.–Canadian relations—as the medical school at McGill University, for example.

The Hays-Fulbright Educational and Cultural Exchange Act of 1961 provides for scholarship programs for American students to study abroad and foreign students to study in the United States. The provisions are applicable to Canada, but there is no student-exchange program with Canada. In many senses, of course, American understanding of Canada may be somewhat greater than it is of some more remote areas of the world, and no doubt this is the major reason why Canada has been excluded by the administration from these student-exchange programs. But American understanding of Canadian affairs is still grossly insufficient to lay the foundation for a model of relations between the nations.

The volume of this exchange should be encouraged by the U.S. Government to make its numbers more compatible with the unique nature of the relations between the two countries—the unique nature of their opportunities for continental cooperation and the unique obligation which a nuclear age imposes upon them to create a model of relations between nations.

Similarly, the United States Government should make every effort to utilize its existing programs of aid to facilitate the growth of Canadian studies programs in U.S. colleges and universities. An effort by the government to make colleges and universities fully aware of the programs available to them in the development of special schools for Canadian-American affairs might help encourage the growth of a more comprehensive approach in this field. In particular, building grants and loans for institutions are available under Titles II and III of the Higher Educational Facilities Act. Title IV of the National Defense Education Act provides for scholarships for students studying the field of international affairs. The State Department might pay special attention to utilizing its university exchange program to allow senior State Department fellows to further their interest in Canadian affairs and at the same time provide impetus for expanded Canadian studies. Similarly, the U.S. Government might wish to consider temporary leaves of absence for some of its officials to take on temporary faculty assignments in the teaching of aspects of Canadian-American relations in educational institutions as they develop.

Perhaps the greatest effort of all, however, must be made in the adult-education and public-affairs efforts outside the classroom. Of American newspapers and periodicals, only *The New York Times* and the *Christian Science Monitor* carry significant coverage of Canadian news. Canadians are frequently surprised to find that the issue of *Time* magazine which they read is a special Canadian edition that is different from that read by Americans. The public-affairs education programs in the United States on television and through the foreign-policy discussion groups organized on a national basis generally ignore Canada, because they are attuned to immediate crises.

The effort must be a broad one undertaken by all those who have an interest in U.S.–Canadian relations, primarily by groups such as the Canadian-American Society of New York and the English-Speaking Union. Their reasons for existence must include the building of a greater American understanding of Canadian interests.

There are, nonetheless, specific measures which can be taken to improve public awareness of Canada in the United States. Under existing legislation, the U.S. administration could and should greatly expand the exchange of journalists and political scientists between Canada and the United States. Under this "foreign-leader" program, journalists and political scientists come to the United States for a period of 60 to 90 days to travel and to study the operations of U.S. newspapers and governmental institutions. Approximately 1,000 "foreign leaders" came to the United States under the program in 1966, and understandably most of these were from the developing countries. Fewer than 60 Canadians have been brought to the United States under the program since its inception in 1961.

More important, however, than the opportunity for Canadians to study in the United States is the opportunity for American journalists and political scientists to study in Canada. While the Hays-Fulbright program permits such an exchange, not a single American has taken part in the program in five years. The U.S. administration should wish to encourage better American understanding of Canadian institutions and interests through increased attention to them in the U.S. communications media. We hope, therefore, that it will give new emphasis to the program of reciprocal exchange of journalists and political scientists between the two countries. One by-product of such an exchange would be the creation of a body of journalistic expertise in the United States on U.S.–Canadian affairs and therefore a greater capacity of U.S. newspaper personnel to understand the significance of Canadian news that comes over the wire services—and hopefully a greater willingness to print it. At the present time, American newsmen are generally so ignorant of U.S.–Canadian affairs that they are unable to judge the significance of news items coming out of Canada, and therefore they make the determination that the safe course is to print nothing.

Second, as we have recommended, the American business community should undertake a broad program of education for its representatives to be sent to Canada. Such a business seminar need not be limited to businessmen anticipating Canadian assignments. The relation of the two economies is so important that American business could undertake profitably for themselves and their nation a self-education course in the Canadian economy, government, history, and culture.

The most essential ingredient of all, however, in the building of a new awareness of Canada in the United States, is the attention given to the subject by the American administration. The sphere of formal education and certainly the sphere of public-affairs adult education are outside the constitutional prerogatives of the federal government in Washington. Nonetheless, as in so many other areas of American culture, the influence of the White House and the government is so potent that its interest could generate a veritable revolution in attention paid to U.S.–Canadian relations not only by public officials but by private citizens as well.

The problem of United States awareness of Canada is acute for the international relations of the two countries. But Canadians have their own problem in relation to education in U.S.–Canadian affairs. One part of the problem is the so-called "brain drain," not just to U.S. scientific and research operations, but to American colleges and universities as well. The building of a competent Canadian college and graduate curriculum must inevitably be a first priority of business for the Canadian and provincial governments if they are to retain promising Canadian students for study in their own country and insure greater employment of their own competent young men and women at home—and if they are to attract interested American students to Canadian universities.

Furthermore, some Canadians have warned their national brethren of a sense of complacency in the fact that Americans know too little of Canada. The Honorable A. D. P. Heeney, former Canadian Ambassador to the United States, co-author of the Merchant-Heeney Report, and presently Chairman of the Canadian Section of the International Joint Commission, has said:

> If we in Canada are to maintain with the United States our traditional relations of practical friendship and partnership, we must, it seems to me, do more to understand the Americans, their way of doing things, their enthusiasms and their prejudices. And as Canada itself is developing into a position in which our opinions count for something, we can no longer rely upon the assumptions of the past and the platitudes of after-dinner oratory.[6]

It is vital to the future of our continent, that the United States and its citizens learn to know Canada and learn to appreciate that Canadians, like any other people, will cooperate freely only on the basis of mutual respect.

169

It is equally vital for the future of the continent that Canadians learn to know the United States—and learn to know that Americans, flamboyant and brash as they sometimes seem, naïve and politically unsophisticated as they often appear, are more the product of blissful ignorance than they are of hostile motives.

There have been theorists in international politics who have suggested that for one people to know another, contrary to the hopes and dreams of men, is to invite international conflict. They suggest that to know a man is to hate him because he is different.

That theory, true or false, contains the seed of the challenge facing this world in the nuclear age. It contains the seed of the challenge facing the North American continent in this second hundred years of U.S.–Canadian relations.

Neither of our two countries can rely on other parts of this war-torn world to lead the way to a new era of peace. We can rely only upon ourselves and upon our devotion to the common principles of our two nations. History has placed the challenge co-equally upon us. Shall this new century of North American relations upon which we are about to embark be the beginning or the end? The opportunity and the obligations are ours. God help all men if we fail.

Notes

Chapter I: One Hundred Years Back, One Hundred Years Forward

[1] As quoted in L. B. Namier, *England in the Age of the American Revolution* (London: Macmillan and Co., Ltd., 1930), p. 324.

[2] See Francis Wharton, ed., *The Revolutionary Diplomatic Correspondence of the United States* (Washington, 1889), Vol. V, pp. 541–42.

[3] U.S. *Congressional Globe*. 41st Cong., 2d Sess. pp. 2887–89.

[4] Oscar D. Skelton, *General Economic History of the Dominion, 1867–1912* (Toronto: The Publishers Association of Canada, Ltd., 1913), p. 102.

[5] Art Buchwald, *Washington Post*, October 24, 1965.

[6] Department of State, *Instructions to United States Ministers*, Volume IX.

Chapter II: Nationalism: Its Virtues, Its Vices

[1] Donald F. Warner, *The Idea of Continental Union, Agitation for the Annexation of Canada to the U.S. 1849–1893* (Lexington, Ky.: University of Kentucky Press, 1960), p. 47.

[2] Hugh L. Keenleyside and Gerald S. Brown, *Canada and the United States* (New York: Alfred A. Knopf, 1952), p. 120.

[3] Hans Kohn, *Idea of Nationalism* (New York: Macmillan, 1945), p. 9.

[4] *Ibid.*, p. 35.

[5] Elie Kedourie, *Nationalism* (rev. ed.; New York: Praeger, 1960), p. 75.

[6] Ramsay Muir, *Nationalism and Internationalism* (London: Constable and Co., Ltd., 1917), p. 222–23.

[7] Thomas Henry Huxley (1825–95), "On University Education."

[8] Hans Kohn, "French Nationalism and Western Unity," in

Mid-twentieth Century Nationalism; the Franklin Memorial Lectures, Vol. XIII, ed. William John Bossenbrook (Detroit: Wayne State University Press, 1965), p. 46.

[9] Kohn, *Idea of Nationalism,* p. 323.

[10] Keenleyside and Brown, *Canada and the United States,* p. 110.

[11] Kohn, *Idea of Nationalism,* p. 282.

[12] From Van Tyne, *The War of Independence: The American Phase,* p. 72, as quoted in Kohn, *Idea of Nationalism,* p. 670.

[13] George Gissing (1857–1903), *The Private Papers of Henry Ryecroft,* I, 16.

Chapter III: Foreign Policy: Power and Obligations

[1] James Eayrs, "The Politics of Disparate Power," an address before the Inter-Collegiate Conference on U.S.–Canadian Relations, Michigan State University, April 2, 1966.

[2] Livingston T. Merchant and A. D. P. Heeney, *Canada and the United States. Principles for Partnership.* U.S. *Department of State Bulletin,* August 2, 1965 (Report dated June 28, 1965), p. 13. Hereinafter referred to as the Merchant-Heeney Report.

[3] *Canadian Weekly Bulletin* (Department of External Affairs, Ottawa, Canada, Vol. 21, No. 17, April 27, 1966), p. 2.

[4] In Ruhl J. Bartlett, ed., *The Record of American Diplomacy* (Third ed.; New York: Alfred A. Knopf, 1954), p. 563.

Chapter IV: Defense: Is There Any Choice?

[1] Melvin Conant, "Canada's Role in Western Defense," *Foreign Affairs,* Vol. 40 (April 1962), p. 435.

[2] Quoted in Brian Crane, *An Introduction to Canadian Defense Policy* (Toronto: Canadian Institute of International Affairs, 1964), p. 4.

[3] *Ibid.,* p. 3.

[4] Paul Hellyer and Lucian Cardin. *White Paper on Defence,* Canadian Department of National Defence, Ottawa, March, 1964, p. 13.

[5] Crane, *An Introduction to Canadian Defense Policy,* p. 2.

[6] Excerpts from Defence Scheme No. 1 are reproduced in

172

James Eayrs, *In Defence of Canada: From the Great War to the Great Depression,* Vol. 1 (Toronto: University of Toronto Press, 1964), pp. 323–28.

[7] James M. Minifie, *Peacemaker or Powder-Monkey* (Canada: McClelland and Stewart, Ltd., 1960), p. 5.

[8] *Ibid.,* p. 20.

[9] Alastair M. Taylor, *For Canada—Both Swords and Ploughshares* (Canadian Institute of International Affairs, 1963), p. 3.

[10] Minifie, *Peacemaker or Powder-Monkey,* p. 9.

[11] A. D. P. Heeney, "Defense and North American Solidarity," Fifth Seminar on U.S.–Canadian Relations at University of Windsor, 1963.

[12] John Paul and Jerome Laulicht, *In Your Opinion,* Vol. 1 (Clarkson, Ontario: Canadian Peace Research Institute, 1963), p. 96.

[13] *Ibid.,* p. 84.

[14] Quoted in James Eayrs, *Northern Approaches: Canada and the Search for Peace* (Toronto: Macmillan, 1961), p. 36.

[15] Paul Martin, "Canada and the Atlantic Community," *External Affairs,* April 1965, p. 124.

[16] In Bartlett, ed., *The Record of American Diplomacy,* p. 563.

Chapter V: Canada in Her Hemisphere

[1] John D. Harbron, *Canada and the Organization of American States* (Canadian-American Committee, 1963), p. 7.

[2] Quoted in *Ibid.,* p. 19.

[3] Quoted in *Ibid.,* p. 20.

[4] *Ibid.,* p. 22.

[5] Editorial by Yvon Turcot, *Montreal Metro Express,* quoted in the *Toronto Daily Star,* September 4, 1965.

[6] A. J. Carley, "The Case for Joining the OAS," *Commentator,* January, 1965, p. 23.

[7] Alexis de Tocqueville, *Democracy in America,* Vol. 2 (New York: Alfred A. Knopf, 1945), pp. 117–18.

Chapter VI: Two Economies or One?

[1] Beland H. Honderich, "United States Investment In Can-

ada," address before the International Press Institute, Quebec City, March 12, 1965.

[2] Robert D. Brown, "Bilateral Chariots—Problems of the Auto Tariff Pact," *The Canadian Forum*, December 1965, p. 198.

[3] Merchant-Heeney Report, p. 10.

[4] *Maclean's Magazine*, June 6, 1964. (Results of survey by Groupe de Recherché Social of Montreal in 1964.)

Chapter VII: Water: The Politics of Supply and Demand

[1] Toronto *Globe and Mail*, September 28, 1965.

[2] Billy M. McCormac, Director of the Geophysics Division at the Illinois Institute of Technology Research, as quoted in the *Washington Post*, April 3, 1966, p. N5.

[3] Thomas F. Bates, Science Adviser, U.S. Department of the Interior, as quoted in *Washington Post*, April 3, 1966, p. N5.

[4] Edmour Germain, "Importing Water from Canada," *Public Utilities Fortnightly*, November 11, 1965, pp. 28–29.

[5] U.S. Senate, Committee on Public Works, Special Subcommittee on Western Water Development. (89th Cong. 2d Sess.), *Western Water Development*. Revised January, 1966, p. 7.

[6] U.S. Senate, 87th Cong., 1st Sess., *Report of the Select Committee on National Water Resources*. Report No. 29, January 30, 1961, pp. 6–9.

[7] Cited by Tom Mahoney, "One Hundred Billion Dollars for Fresh Water?" *American Legion Magazine*, September, 1965, p. 39.

[8] *Ibid.*

[9] Merchant-Heeney Report, p. 11.

[10] Arthur Laing, as quoted in *Toronto Daily Star*, October 4, 1965.

[11] *Canada Yearbook, 1965*, Official Statistical Annual of the Resources, History, Institutions and Social and Economic Conditions of Canada (Ottawa: Dominion Bureau of Statistics, 1965).

[12] *Toronto Daily Star*, March 11, 1966.

[13] T. W. Kierans, *The Kierans Plan* (Sudbury, Ontario: March 21, 1960).

[14] North American Water and Power Alliance, Ralph M. Parsons Co. Brochure 606–2934–19, p. 4.

[15] Jack Davis, "Energy in its Continental Setting," Sixth Seminar on Canadian-American Relations at University of Windsor, 1964, p. 178.

Chapter VIII: The Continental Institutions

[1] Tim Creery, Southam News Services, Ottawa, Ontario, "Energy Resources: The North American Political Concept," Fifth U.S.–Canadian Relations Seminar at the University of Windsor, 1964.

[2] Governor Hart to Secretary of State Hughes, Telegram, July 26, 1921, National Archives, U. S. Department of State File 711, 428/645.

[3] Merchant-Heeney Report, p. 8.

[4] J. L. MacCallum, "The International Joint Commission," *Canadian Geographical Journal*, Vol. LXXII, No. 3, (March 1966).

[5] Lawrence J. Burpee, "A Successful Experiment in International Relations," *International Joint Commission Papers* (Ottawa), 1929, p. 41.

[6] Lawrence J. Burpee, "Insurance for Peace," *International Joint Commission Papers* (Ottawa), 1929, p. 64.

[7] Joseph Chirakaikaran Chacko, *The International Joint Commission* (New York: Columbia University Press, 1932), p. 374.

Chapter IX: Mobility: The Symbol of Progress

[1] Keenleyside and Brown, *Canada and the United States*, p. 305.

[2] An address by Honorable René Tremblay, Minister of Citizenship and Immigration, before the Richelieu Club of Quebec, March 17, 1964.

[3] Canadian Government Immigration Service, Press Release, February 15, 1966.

[4] *Ibid.*

[5] *Business Week*, May 22, 1965, pp. 110–14.

[6] Maurice Davie, *World Immigration* (New York: Macmillan, 1949), p. 212.

[7] Bern Keating, "Louisiana's French Speaking Cajunland," *National Geographic*, March, 1966.

[8] From a June 1944 letter from Adolphe Robert, President

General of the Association Canado-Americaine, as quoted in Francis J. Brown and Joseph S. Roucek, ed., *One America* (New York: 1952), p. 342.

[9] Address by Honorable René Tremblay, March 17, 1964.

[10] *Ibid.*

[11] Michael Barkway, *Turning Point for Immigration?* (Canadian Institute for International Affairs, 1957).

[12] *Business Week*, May 22, 1965.

[13] *Ottawa Journal*, November 26, 1965.

[14] *Toronto Daily Star*, August 27, 1965.

Chapter X: An Appalling Ignorance

[1] *American Heritage*, December 1965, p. 4.

[2] Arthur A. Hauck, "Some Educational Factors Affecting the Relations Between Canada and the United States," Doctoral dissertation, 1932.

[3] Robin W. Winks, "A Century of Misunderstanding: Canadian-American Cultural Relations," *International Educational and Cultural Exchange*, Fall, 1965, pp. 6–18.

[4] *Ibid.*, p. 6.

[5] Robin W. Winks, "Thirty Years After: Canadian History in the Universities of the U.S." *Canadian Historical Review*, 1959, pp. 38–50.

[6] A. D. P. Heeney, "The Americans—How Well Do We Really Know Them?" an address to the Women's Canadian Club of Montreal, February 7, 1955.

Appendix

Results of Test Administered in March/April 1966 to 1,000 Canadian and 1,000 U.S. High School Seniors

Question	*Per Cent Correct Answers*	
	Canadian Students	U.S. Students
1. What is the capital of (the United States) (Canada)?	99.1	32.9
2. Who is the (President of the United States) (Prime Minister of Canada)?	99.9	32.8
3. What political party does the (President) (Prime Minister) represent?	69.4	13.3
4. Who was the leader of the opposition party in the last (United States) (Canadian) election?	76.2	14.5
5. Name two (states in the United States) (Canadian provinces).	98.8	68.0
6. What is the name of the U.S.–Canadian defense organization?	25.5	7.0
7. Is (the United States) (Canada) a member of NATO?	85.5	73.1
8. Is (the United States) (Canada) a member of the OAS?	70.2	46.1
9. Who is the (Canadian Ambassador to the United States) (United States Ambassador to Canada)?	1.4	0

10. What is the official language of (the United States) (Canada)?   98.6   10.5

11. What is the population of (the United States) (Canada)?   42.3   13.5

Index

Index

181

184

186

187

Organization of American States, *see* OAS
Ottawa (Ont.), 25, 28, 62, 148, 159, 164-65

Pakistan, 35, 137
Pan American Institute of Geography and History, 80
Pan American Radio Office, 80
Pan-American Union, 78-79
Parliament, Canadian, 21, 26-27, 54, 132-34
  Kennedy's speech to, 79, 86
Pearson, Lester, 52, 81, 159
Pembina River, 136
Permanent Joint Board of Defense, 65, 67, 69-70, 130
Philadelphia (Pa.), 25
Phoenix (Ariz.), 115
Poland, 34, 151
Poleson, Robert, 149
Political divisions, 23-25
Pollution, 113-18, 120, 134
Population, 18, 23-24, 162; *see also* Immigration
Portland (Ore.), 25, 63
Power, hydroelectric, 98, 123-24
Powers, separation of, 25-27
Punta del Este Conference (Dec. 1961), 86-87

Quebec, 25, 62, 110, 148, 160
  immigration and, 144, 146, 152

"Rationalization," economic, 97-98, 108
Red River (of the North), 136
Religion, 21, 31, 94, 149-52
Responsibility (obligation), 69, 71, 99

Canadian, 45-46, 51-58, 121-22
  of U.S., 104, 118
  economic, 102, 106-7
  political, 47-51, 89-90
Ricker College (Houlton, Me.), 165
Rio Grande Valley, 115
Ritchie, A. E., 161
Rivers, 24-25, 115, 119
  diversion of, 120, 122, 126
  See also specific rivers
Rocky Mountain Trench Reservoir (B.C.), 124
Roebuck, Carl A., 149
Roosevelt, Franklin D., 61, 79
Root, Elihu, 135
Russia, *see* Soviet Union

St. Lawrence Seaway, 28, 113, 122, 124, 126
  regulation of, 134, 136
St. Louis (Mo.), 25
Salt Lake City (Utah), 115
Senate, U.S., 54, 116, 119, 130
Separation of powers, 25-27
Sewage, 94, 113, 120, 139
Smoot-Hawley Tariff (1930), 101
South America, *see* Latin America
Soviet Union, 21-22, 34-35, 51, 87
  economic aid from, 73, 95
  as nuclear power, 48, 65, 68, 70, 72
Spain, 34
Spanish-American War, 38
Standard of living, 18
State, Department of (U.S.), 71, 95-96, 130, 133, 166-67
State boundaries, U.S., 23-25

Statute of Westminister (1931), 78
Student-exchange programs, 165-68
Suspicion of U.S. motives
  Canadian, 29, 111-12, 121, 147
  Latin American, 37, 89, 95

Taylor, Alastair, 67
Time (magazine), 167
Tobago, 77, 80
Tocqueville, Alexis de, 94-95
Toronto Daily Star, 53-54
Toronto Globe and Mail, 71, 112
Towns, *see* Cities and towns
Trade, foreign, 82
  with Communist countries, 56, 106-7
  U.S.-Canadian, 81, 99-102, 108-11, 125
    regulations, 101, 108-9, 127, 131-32
Trading with the Enemy Act (1917), 107
Transportation, 36, 94, 113, 122, 125
  growth of, 18-20, 24
Trinidad, 77, 80
Truman, Harry S, 48
Tupper Report (Sept. 1965), 22-23, 59, 102-3, 107, 112, 131
Turkish nationalism, 34

United Nations, 17, 64, 76, 80
  Canadian contributions to, 41-42
  Inter-American system vs., 83-84, 87
  peacekeeping efforts of, 53-54, 74, 140

U.S. joins, 33, 39
U.S. policy toward, 50-51

Vancouver (Wash.), 25
Viet Nam war, 39, 49, 93
  Canadian responsibility toward, 52, 54-55
  U.S. opinion divided over, 57

War of 1812, 38, 144, 164
Wars, 32-33, 60, 92-93, 126; *see also* Defense; *specific wars*
Washington, D.C., 24-25, 164
Washington State, 130
Water, 98, 112-26, 134-39
  plans for sharing, 118-19, 121-26, 138
  U.S. shortage of, 113-17, 121
Water Resources Council, 119
Welles, Sumner, 79, 82
Western U.S., water problem in, 45
White papers, 61; *see also* Tupper Report
Whitman, Walt, "Specimen Days," 109-10
Wilson, Woodrow, 30, 33, 39
Winnipeg (Man.), 17, 62
Winters, Robert H., 103
World Affairs Councils, 164
World War I, 32-33, 39, 41, 56, 78, 101
  lessons of, 62-63
World War II, 33, 37, 41, 56-57, 78, 101
  cooperative defense planning for, 62-64
  nuclear attacks in, 71

Yakima Valley (Wash.), 115

About the Authors

The two authors of our book bring to this major effort the wisdom of many years of dedication to the pursuit of peace among nations.

Stanley R. Tupper was in 1966 personally chosen by President Johnson as the United States Commissioner General for United States participation in the Canadian Universal and International Exhibition with the rank of Ambassador. Previously, he served three terms as Congressman from Maine. He has been a member of the Canada-United States Interparliamentary Group for six consecutive years.

Douglas L. Bailey, now serving as Public Affairs Consultant to Republican Members of Congress, was in 1964 the Associate Director of Foreign Policy Research in the presidential campaign of Governor Nelson A. Rockefeller. Until that year, he held two important posts at Harvard University: Research Associate in its Center for International Affairs, and Associate in its Defense Studies Program.